COLLINS
WALK THE CORNISH COASTAL PATH

by John H N Mason

GW00420263

HarperCollins*Publishers*

Published by Collins
An imprint of HarperCollins*Publishers*
77-85 Fulham Palace Road
London W6 8JB

Copyright © HarperCollins*Publishers* 1998
Text © John H.N. Mason 1995
Maps © Bartholomew 1995

First published by Bartholomew 1989
Revised 1990, 1991, 1995
Reprinted 1997
This new edition 1998

All rights reserved. No part of this publication may be reproduced
stored in a retrieval system, or transmitted in any form or by any
means, electronic, mechanical, photocopying, recording, or
otherwise, without the prior written permission of the Publisher
and copyright owner.

The landscape is changing all the time. While every care has
been taken in the preparation of this guide, the Publisher accepts
no responsibility whatsoever for any loss, damage, injury or
inconvenience sustained or caused as a result of using this guide.

Printed in Hong Kong

ISBN 0 00 448 701 X

89/5/64

CONTENTS

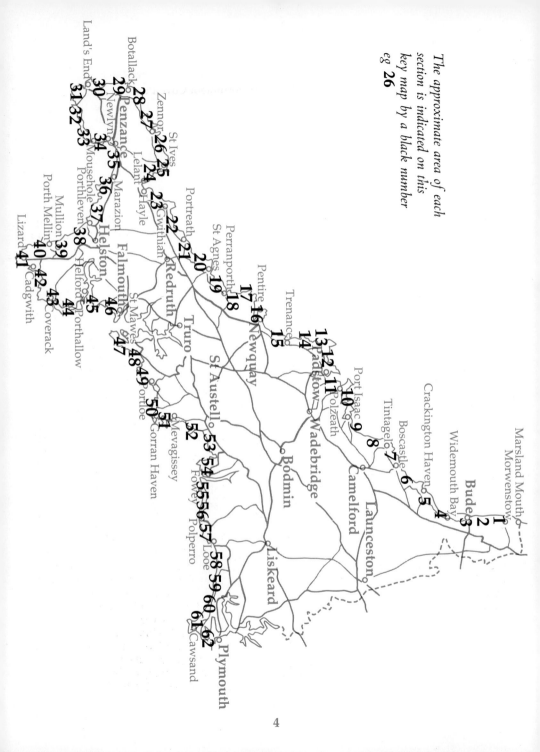

The approximate area of each
section is indicated on this
key map by a black number
eg **26**

Marsland Mouth
Morwenstow
1
2
Bude 3
Widemouth Bay
4
5
Crackington Haven
6
Boscastle
Tintagel **7**
8
Port Isaac **9**
10
Polzeath
11
12
13
Padstow
14
15
Trenance
Pentire **16**
17
18
St Agnes **19**
Perranporth
20
Portreath **21**
22
23
Gwithian
24
25
St Ives
26
Zennor
27
28
Botallack
Land's End
29
30
31 32
33
Newlyn
Penzance
34
35
36
Mousehole
37
Marazion
Lelant
Hayle
Redruth
Truro
Newquay
Trenance
St Mawes
47
48 49
Portloe
50
51
Gorran Haven
Mevagissey
52
St Austell
53
54
55 56
Fowey
57
Polperro
Looe
58
59 60
61 62
Cawsand
Plymouth
Liskeard
Bodmin
Wadebridge
Camelford
Launceston
Falmouth
Helston
Porthallow
Porthleven
Helford
45
46
Mullion **39**
Porth Mellin
40
Lizard **41**
Cadgwith **42**
43
Coverack
44
38

4

1 THE CORNISH COASTAL PATH

There could be no better way to experience the varied coasts and landscapes of Cornwall, away from the traffic and bustle of crowds, than to follow all or part of the Cornish Coastal Path from the wild rocky coasts of the north via sandy coves, intriguing villages, and long beaches to eventually arrive at Plymouth Sound.

The National Parks Act of 1949 provided for a number of long-distance footpaths throughout the country, now known as National Trails. The longest of these is the South-West Coast Path, which runs along the coast from Minehead in Somerset to Poole Harbour in Dorset. This guide describes the entire Cornish stretch of the path.

Most of the Cornish coast has been designated as one of the 'Heritage Coasts' of England and, as such, is subject to special measures of conservation. The Countryside Commission, which works through the local authorities, appoints 'Heritage Coast Officers' for the regions involved. For information on the Heritage Coasts, apply to the Countryside Commission, Bridge House, Sion Place, Bristol BS8 4AS. The South-West Way Association, which furthers the interests of walkers on the Coastal Path, publishes an annual guide for its members with up-to-date information on the Path. Details are available from 1 Orchard Drive, Kingskerswell, Newton Abbot, Devon TQ12 5DG.

Each part of the route in this guide is graded section by section according to the type of terrain to be covered. Most sections can be negotiated without much difficulty although the elderly and those not so active should consider carefully before tackling the stretches shown as 'strenuous' in the text.

The Path is often rocky and, even on the least strenuous of sections, good, strong, well-tried, comfortable walking boots are a 'must'. They not only help you to maintain a sure-footed grip but, worn with woollen socks, they reduce the risk of blistered and tired feet.

Cornwall has a good weather record and, with normal good fortune, you will probably experience reasonable walking weather. You should, however, be prepared for rain and wind so lightweight rainwear is important. A loose-fitting waterproof, knee-length jacket with a hood should keep you dry. Waterproof overtrousers are also useful. In hot sun, remember to keep your head and neck protected. Your motto should be 'Travel light!'.

2 HOW TO USE THIS GUIDE

The purpose of this guide is to enable the reader not only to find his or her way easily and accurately, section by section, along the full length of the Cornish Coastal Path but also to provide additional information in a most convenient form that can be of the greatest help in planning and while walking. The sketch maps take the work out of following the path and navigating your route. Nevertheless, a good 1:100 000 map showing the line of the path is an excellent complement to this guide, especially

Symbols

	Feature (see text)		
	Access to path	(P)	Parking
—	Path	(T)	Toilets
▪▪▪	Alternative		Telephone
---▷	Other footpaths		Shop
▶	Steeply up		Meals
▷	Steeply down		Light Refreshments
++++	Fence		Pub
∞∞∞	Hedge or wall		Pub specially recommended
S	Stream		Bed and breakfast lower to medium price range
,G,	Gorse		Bed and breakfast more expensive
,B,	Bracken		
)(	Footbridge	(all)	all above facilities
	Rocks near path	YH	Youth Hostel
	Paving stones	□	Open all year
△	'Trig' point		Camp site
NT	National Trust		Overnight pitch if permission obtained
C G	Coast Guard		
	Shingle or sand		Church with tower
	Rocks or boulders		Church with spire
	Good beach	(F)	Ferry
	Swimming		Railway Station
	Surfing		Bus station
	Lighthouse		Bus stop
	Incline		Birds or flowers

if you are seeking more detailed information on access or are interested in leaving the path for short excursions inland.

The key to symbols used on the maps in this guide is shown opposite and is worth examining as the maps provide a great deal of invaluable information on types of terrain and facilities available. Gradient indications are given on the line of the path and guidance is given in places where there may otherwise be difficulty in finding the way.

Other helpful features are the symbols marking the approximate location of refreshment facilities as well as guest houses, hotels, hostels and camp-sites. The texts accompanying the maps serve to amplify the information on the route itself. The official Path is indicated by a solid green line and alternative paths are shown by a broken line.

Distances On the right hand side of each map, an indication of approximate mileages is given. Note: 1 mile=1.6093km. At the beginning of each section, the distance to be walked is shown as well as the cumulative distance from the Devon border at Marsland Mouth. Approximate metric equivalents are also given.

Access to the Path The guide endeavours to cater for everyone with an interest in the Path; the more serious walkers may wish to spend a week or fortnight walking every day, whereas there may be some whose interest extends only to an afternoon's stroll or a day's walk and would therefore prefer to select a particular stretch of the Path. To help in this, the guide includes in the maps the most convenient access points to the Path, indicated by a green arrow. Adjacent car-parking facilities, where available, are also shown.

Bus services Bus services in Cornwall are not plentiful but, where they exist, they keep well to timetable. Most are operated by Western National but there are also smaller private companies running services that can be most useful. Information on the Western National services is obtainable from their main office at Pydar Street, Truro. Tel. Truro (01872) 40404. They can also put you in touch with the private companies. The Cornwall County Council publish annually a complete timetable guide to all public transport including bus services, public and private, as well as rail travel, air connections, the Scilly Isles steamer and ferries. Copies can be obtained through the Western National office. Address as above. They are also on sale at Tourist Information Offices in Cornwall.

It should be kept in mind that many services run only in the summer season or on certain days of the week. Always check the timetables carefully.

Bathing This is often dangerous, particularly for children or non-swimmers so pay attention to warning signs and be guided by flags and lifeguards.

Tides When walking the Cornish Coastal Path, a knowledge of the state of the tide on a particular day is often useful. On a stretch in this book, you may wish to wade an estuary and this can only be done at low tide.

The information given below will enable you, with the help of your newspaper, to determine the approximate time of high and low water. You may also be able to buy local tide tables at newsagents.

Most national daily newspapers give the time of high water at London Bridge (usually with the weather details). By adding to this the average time difference in hours and minutes given below, you can calculate the approximate time of high water at the places mentioned. For intermediate places, it will be at some time between the two places each side. Low water is approximately six hours after high water.

	hrs	mins
Budehaven	3	55
Padstow	3	43
Newquay	3	33
St Ives	3	33
Newlyn (Penzance)	3	13
Lizard Point	3	15
Falmouth	3	35
Mevagissey	3	53
Fowey	3	53
Looe	3	55
Plymouth	4	13

Refreshments Where possible, an indication is given on the map of where refreshments may be obtained en route. Telephone numbers, where appropriate, are given below. It is worth remembering, however, that many places are only open June to August.

Accommodation The accommodation shown in the guide has been selected for its position close to the Path and its capacity to provide overnight bed and breakfast for walkers. Accommodation has been divided into two price categories (see Symbols p.6). However, when making reservations, always check costs. The telephone number for each establishment is given below and the location has been indicated as near as is possible on the map in relation to the Path. If you have not made an advance reservation, you should decide your target for the following day and then book the nearest accommodation to it. If, for some reason, the guest house, hostel or hotel cannot give lodgings, the proprietor will probably be able to suggest a suitable alternative nearby. Always make clear whether or not an evening meal is required and try to give some indication of expected time of arrival. Two letters on the map after the name of the establishment indicate the period the accommodation is available e.g. AO=April to October, SM=September to March. □ indicates open throughout the year including the winter months. However, this could be subject to many local variables so it is worth obtaining advance confirmation. On the map, GH=guest house and CS=camp-site.

Useful telephone numbers Hotels, guest houses, camp-sites, youth hostels and Tourist Information Offices as shown on the maps (please note that, for some local calls, the code may differ depending on where you are. Check the notice in the telephone box).

Section

1	Hermitage, Welcombe Mouth	(01288) 331258
	Ravine camp-site, Yealmouth	(01288) 331473
	Dene Farm, Morwenstow	,(01288) 331330
2	Atlantic Park Leisure Park, Bude	(01288) 352563
3	Mornish Hotel, Bude	(01288) 352972
	Tourist Information, Bude	(01288) 354240
	Meva Gwin, Upton	(01288) 352347
	Upper Lynstone Farm camp-site	(01288) 352017
4	Widemouth Bay camp-site	(01288) 361208

Penhalt Farm camp-site,
Millook (01288) 361210
5 Coombe Barton Inn (01840) 230345
Crackington Haven camp-site (01840) 230365
6 Lower Pennycrocker Farm
camp-site (01840) 250257
Trevique Farm (01840) 230418
7 Youth Hostel, Boscastle (01840) 250287
Wellington Hotel, Boscastle (01840) 250203
Tolcarne Holiday Hotel,
Boscastle (01840) 250654
Sunnyside, Boscastle (01840) 250453
Trewethett camp-site (01840) 770533
Pengenna Hotel, Tintagel (01840) 770223
Penallick Hotel, Tintagel (01840) 770296
8 Youth Hostel, Tintagel (01840) 770334
9 Port Gaverne Hotel (01208) 880244
10 Shipwright Inn, Port Isaac (01208) 880305
12 Roskarnon Hotel, Rock (01208) 862785
Old Custom House Inn, Padstow (01841) 532359
Old Ship Hotel, Padstow (01841) 532357
Sea Food Restaurant, Padstow (01841) 532485
River View, Padstow (01841) 532767
Tourist Information, Padstow (01841) 533449
13 Higher Harlyn Farm camp-site,
Harlyn (01841) 520022
14 Youth Hostel, Treyarnon Bay (01841) 520322
Bay House Hotel, Porthcothan (01841) 520472
15 Gluvian camp-site,
Mawgan Porth (01637) 860373
Seavista Hotel, Mawgan Porth (01637) 860276
White Lodge guest house
Mawgan Porth (01637) 860512
16 Trevelgue Park camp-site (016373) 873475
17 Mellanvrane Hotel (016373) 872593
Tourist Information, Newquay (01637) 871345
Youth Hostel, Newquay (01637) 876381
Goose Rock Hotel, W. Pentire (01637) 830755
Treworgans Farm camp-site (¾
mile/1¼km) inland from P.Joke) (01637) 830200
18 Park View, Perranporth (01872) 573009
Youth Hostel, Perranporth (01872) 573812
Tourist Information, Perranporth (01872)573368
19 Driftwood Spars, St Agnes (01872) 552428
20 Beacon Cottage Farm camp-site,
St Agnes (01872) 552347
Porpoise Inn, Porthtowan (01209) 890384
Beach Hotel, Porthtowan (01209) 890228
Kernou Hotel, Porthtowan (01209) 890386
21 Glenfeadon House, Portreath (01209) 842650
22 Magor Farm camp-site,
nr Portreath (01209) 713367
24 Beachside camp-site, Hayle (01736) 753080
25 Chy-An-Gweal camp-site,
Carbis Bay (01736) 796257

Ayr Park camp-site (01736) 795855
Sheaf of Wheat Inn, St Ives (01736) 797130
Grey Mullet, St Ives (01736) 796635
Kandahar, St Ives (01736) 796183
Tourist Information, St Ives (01736) 796297
26 Trevalgan Farm (01736) 796433
27 Trewey-Vean Farm, Zennor (01736) 796919
29 Mrs Old's St John's House (01736) 788550
Trewellard Hotel (01736) 788634
Levant House camp-site,1
Pendeen (01736) 788795
Count House Restaurant (01736) 788588
Manor Farm, Botallack (01736) 788525
Trevaylor camp-site, Botallack (01736) 787016
Boscean Country Hotel (01736) 788748
Queens Arms, Botallack (01736)788316
30 Youth Hostel, Land's End (01736) 788437
31 Old Success Inn, Sennen (01736) 871232
State House Hotel, Land's End (01736) 871501
32 Treen Post Office camp-site (01736) 810526
Mrs George, Fernleigh (01736) 810324
33 Tremeneth guest house, Lamorna (01736) 731367
Lamorna Cove Hotel, Lamorna (01736) 731411
34 Raginnis Farm, Mousehole
(see map) (01736) 731333
Lobster Pot, Mousehole (01736) 731251
Ship Inn, Mousehole (01736) 731234
Kings Arms, Paul (01736) 731224
35 Yacht Inn, Penzance (01736) 62787
Longboat Inn, Penzance (01736) 64137
Blue Seas guest house, Penzance (01736) 64744
Youth Hostel, Penzance (01736) 62666
Tourist Information, Penzance (01736) 62207
Mounts Bay camp-site (01736) 64160
Cutty Sark Hotel, Marazion (01736) 710334
36 Kenneggy Cove Farm camp-site (01736) 763453
37 Praa Sands Hotel, Praa Sands (01736) 762438
Pengersick camp-site, Praa Sands (01736) 762201
38 Harbour Hotel, Porthleven (01326) 573876
Tye Rock Hotel, Porthleven (01326) 572695
39 Marconi guest house, Mullion (01326) 240483
Old Inn, Mullion (01326) 240240
Mullion Cove Hotel,
Mullion Cove (01326) 240328
40 Teneriffe Farm camp-site,
Predannack (01326) 240293
41 Parc Brawse House, Lizard (01326) 290466
Housel Bay Hotel, Lizard (01326) 290417
Cadgwith Cove Inn, Cadgwith (01326) 290513
42 Sea Acres camp-site,
Kennack Sands (01326) 290665
43 Little Trevothan Park camp-site (01326) 280260
Youth Hostel, Coverack (01326) 280687
44 White Hart Inn, St Keverne (01326) 280325
Valley View, Porthallow (01326) 280596

8

45	Tregildry Hotel, Gillan	(01326) 231378
	Landrivick Farm, Helford	
	1¾ miles/2¾km (transport	
	provided if advised)	(01326) 231249
	Riverside, Helford	(01326)231443
46	West Bay Hotel	(01326) 250447
	Penrose Farm, Maen Porth	(01326) 250202
	Youth Hostel, Falmouth	(01326) 311435
	Tremorvan camp-site,	
	Swanpool, Falmouth	(01326) 312103
	Bradgate guest house, Falmouth	(01326) 314108
	Harbour guest house, Falmouth	(01326) 311344
	Tourist Information, Falmouth	(01326) 312300
47	St Mawes Hotel, St Mawes	(01326) 270266
	Green Lantern, St Mawes	(01326) 270502
	Braganza, St Mawes	(01326) 270281
48	Pendower Hotel, Gerrans Bay	(01872) 501257
	Trengerein, Porthscatho	(01872) 580336
49	Ship Inn, Portloe	(01872) 501356
	Lugger Hotel, Portloe	(01872) 501322
	Tregain Tea Room, Portloe	(01872) 501252
50	Youth Hostel, Boswinger	(01726) 843234
51	Smuggler's House,	
	Gorran Haven	(01726) 843228
	Llawnroc Hotel, Gorran Haven	(01726) 843461
	Trelispen camp-site,	
	Gorran Haven	(01726) 843501
	Treleaven Farm, Mevagissey	(01726) 842413
	Cawtes Cottage guest house,	
	Mevagissey	(01726) 842396
	Ship Inn, Mevagissey	(01726) 843324
	Trevalsa Court Hotel,	
	Mevagissey	(01726) 842468
53	Trewhiddle Estate camp-site	(01726) 67011
	Pier House Hotel, Charlestown	(01726) 75272
	Porth Avallen Hotel	(01726)812802
54	Par Sands camp-site, Par Sands	(01726)812868
55	Youth Hostel, Fowey (Golant)	(01726) 833507
	Tourist Information, Fowey	(01726)833616
56	Crumplehorn Inn, Polperro	(01503) 72348
	Mill House Hotel, Polperro	(01503) 72362
57	Talland Barton camp-site	(01503) 72429
	Talland Bay Hotel, Talland Bay	(01503) 72667
	Hannafore Point, Looe	(01503) 263273
	Westcliffe Guest House, Looe	(01503) 262927
	Harbour View, Looe	(01503)262701
	The Ship, Looe	(01503) 263124
	Tourist Information, Looe	(01503) 262072
58	Bokenver Farm	(01503) 240342
	Blue Haven guest house, Seaton	(01503) 250310
60	Finnygook Inn, Crafthole	(01503) 30338
	Liscawn Inn, Crafthole	(01503) 30231
62	Contenders Hotel, Kingsand	(01752) 822278
	Kynance Hotel, Plymouth	(01752) 266821
	Tourist Information, Plymouth	(01752) 264849

3 CORNWALL

Cornwall has been known for over a thousand years as a place of almost magical attraction. Troubadours in France and Germany sang its praises. A host of story-tellers, among them Tennyson and Wagner, have been inspired by dramatic tales of King Arthur and knightly chivalry and love, in their incomparable setting of Cornish cliff and rock, battered by boiling seas.

Cornwall is not only a land of austere grandeur. The southern coast provides gentler slopes, green fields and quiet bays of fine sand. The peaceful sheltered coves in the north are perfect for the holiday-maker and the scenic beauty is without comparison. The fishing villages are a photographer's delight and full of interest. Wild flowers and a variety of bird life are found in profusion.

The people of Cornwall are of very special descent. They pride themselves on their pre-Roman Celtic stock. Their Cornish language was spoken until the 1700s and local directories still contain hundreds of names starting with Tre-, Pol- or Pen- testifying to their ancient origins.

The Cornish are very proud of their 'separate' heritage and are proud to boast of it to the 'travellers down from England'.

4 A SHORT HISTORY OF CORNWALL

In the warmer conditions after the Ice Age, all Cornwall except the highest ground became covered by forest. Mesolithic (Mid Stone Age) Man, who inhabited the land, was probably a nomadic hunter and fisherman.

In about 3500BC Neolithic (New Stone Age) settlers, using a variety of stone tools and weapons, arrived from the Atlantic seaboard of Europe. They knew how to make pottery, how to raise crops and rear flocks and herds. Their boats were possibly of the coracle type still used in Ireland.

They founded settlements in forest clearings and used axes made of greenstone. Monuments of the Neolithic and Early Bronze Age people are the stone chamber tombs used for communal burials, known as 'quoits'. Surmounted by huge stone slabs and covered originally by earthen mounds, there are a number to be found near the north Coast Path, a typical example being Zennor Quoit near St Ives. At Carn Gloose (see p.48), there is an 'entrance' tomb.

In about 2000BC the Beaker Folk, of a more advanced culture, arrived. Their name refers to the type of pottery they made. They introduced the bow and arrow for hunting and fighting, and brought with them the knowledge of the working of metals. It was they who erected the imposing stone circles and standing stones all over Cornwall which were probably of religious significance. Examples near the south Coast Path, not far from Lamorna, are the Merry Maidens and the Pipers (see p.51)

The discovery that tin added to copper made more effective tools and weapons ushered in the Bronze Age (c1500BC to 700BC) and brought a new development to Cornwall, marked principally by a growth in trade with Ireland and the Continent. Metal goods, bronze axes and tools were exchanged for ornaments and other articles. In Truro Museum there is a beautiful gold neck-ornament from Ireland, found at Harlyn on the north Coast Path. It was probably traded for ore or metal. A gold cup buried with a chieftain in east Cornwall was of a Greek pattern, indicating that trade links may have extended to Greece. Bronze Age man lived mainly by agriculture: at Gwithian, on the north Coast Path near Hayle, plough and spade marks from the Bronze Age have been found.

The next migrants to reach southern Britain in about 700BC were the Iron Age Celts from north-west Europe, from whose language Cornish and the other Celtic languages were derived. They introduced the iron-making process. Organised in clans, they formed alliances under kings and were constantly warring among themselves, using iron weapons. Characteristic signs of the Celtic occupation are the hill forts and cliff castles (fortifications) of Cornwall. On the Coast Path between Land's End and Looe there are as many as 10 cliff castles. They all feature a steep headland fortified by one or more ramparts, usually built across the narrowest part of the promontory — Treryn Dinas (see p.50) is a good example. Their role was probably to provide a defensive foothold on first landing or a 'rear base' for new settlements. It is suggested that the name Cornwall was derived from the Cornish word Cornovii meaning cliff castles (Corn meaning promontory).

Trade increased with the Continent. In one of the first written records of Cornwall, the Greek historian Diodorus Siculus in the 1st century BC notes that the tin, after smelting, was taken on waggons to Ictis (St Michael's Mount) at low tide and then by sea to Brittany, then over land to the Mediterranean; and this is supported by other evidence. In Truro Museum is a 158lb (72kg) ingot of tin — in the H-shape mentioned by Diodorus Siculus — that was dredged up off St Mawes.

The Celts became famous for their metal work, producing bronze utensils and ornaments. A bronze bowl made in south-west Britain has been found in a chieftain's grave in Poland. Some of their settlements were 'courtyard villages' with a number of huts built around a courtyard. The excavations at Chysauster, 4 miles (6½km) north of Penzance, give a good idea of the lay-out. The fogous — underground stone food storage chambers (see p.47) — originate from this period.

The legions of the Roman Emperor Claudius landed in Britain in AD43. Four years later after subduing the Celtic and pre-Celtic population of the south west, then known as the Dumnonii, the Romans erected a fort at Isca Dumnoniorum (Exeter) but do not appear to have bothered much about the small isolated communities in Cornwall. Roman remains are sparse, consisting of one or two poorly constructed villas and a few milestones, probably marking roads to the tin mines which we know were exploited as Imperial property. The Celtic chieftains became Romanised but there is evidence that life continued much the same as before the conquest.

After the departure of the Romans in AD410 the Romano-Britons, mainly Celts, were pushed by the Anglo Saxons into the Welsh mountains and to Cornwall. Many of those reaching Cornwall then crossed to their fellow-Celts in north-west France, giving it the name 'Brittany', but others remained, forming a Celtic community in Cornwall. As in Wales, their Roman Christianity survived, and of course, their language, while English became the tongue of the rest of England. It was not until 500 years later that the Saxon King Athelstan finally conquered the Cornish.

The 5th and 6th centuries were remarkable for the number of Welsh, Irish and Breton Christian missionaries who came over to Cornwall, giving so many unusual saints' names to churches, towns and villages, such as St Beryan, St Keverne, St Levan with St Levan's Well, and St Winwalloe. Some of these missionaries founded monasteries, some ministered to their flock from small chapels or cells. The remains of the monastery on the cliff-edge at Tintagel leave an impression of grandeur and simplicity.

Our knowledge of this period is derived from old manuscripts describing the lives of these saints and from the memorial stones and crosses found in Cornwall. These are memorials to local chieftains and the inscriptions in Latin indicate that something, at least, of Roman culture still survived. The Selus Stone in St Just church is a good example.

Cornwall had only been a part of Anglo-Saxon England for just over 100 years when William the Conqueror landed at Pevensey Bay. By 1072 Cornwall was in Norman hands. The first towns in Cornwall began to spring up, some around the Norman castles, as in the case of Truro, others as markets founded by traders in the wake of the Conquest, some around the monasteries. Other outward signs of Norman rule began to appear: notably Norman churches, built on or near the sites of Cornish or Saxon chapels or cells revered by the Cornish. Towednack church near St Ives is almost entirely Norman.

Tin continued to be extracted from alluvial sources and these 'stanneries', working under a Warden, received royal charters from the early 13th century. The tin was tested at official 'coinage' towns: Truro, Bodmin, Lostwithiel, Liskeard, and Helston. It was then taken by sea to London where it was in demand for making pewter for drinking vessels and plates.

As with the rest of England, the structure of Cornish life was feudal, the landed gentry building substantial farmhouses. Despite the predominance of Norman institutions, the Cornish still retained their rugged individuality. With their separate language, the inhabitants of Cornwall were a fiercely independent people, although they played a full part in the life of the nation. Cornish ships and seafarers were invaluable in the Hundred Years War; Sir John Trelawny of the famous Cornish family, with other Cornish knights and their bands of Cornishmen, fought at Agincourt. They raided the French shore, being raided in turn. Fowey and Looe were both burnt by the French. With the War over, the Cornish were not above a little piracy.

The Cornish gave Henry VII their support, probably because of his Celtic origin. They rebelled, however, aginst his taxes and reached Blackheath, 7 miles (11¼ km) from London before they were beaten by royal levies, and their leaders executed.

The growing prosperity and settled conditions, coupled with the religious fervour of the Cornish, resulted in a burst of church rebuilding. We owe many of the beautiful 15th-century Cornish churches which remain today to this period. The Cornishman's Catholic faith had a rude shock when Henry VIII ordered the dissolution of the monasteries. Even more repellent was the liturgy in English, largely an unknown tongue, in place of the familiar Latin and Cornish. Once again the Cornish marched, this time with the Devon men, to lay siege to Protestant Exeter. This, too, was unsuccessful, with many killed and the leaders were put to death.

Cornish ships and men took part in the defeat of the Armada, and were involved in the continuing struggle between Spain and England: Penzance and neighbouring Mousehole and Newlyn were burned by the Spaniards in raids in 1595.

The Cornish gentry were wholeheartedly Royalist in the Civil War, and their men followed them into battle.

Cornish Royalist contingents scored a victory

near Bude and elsewhere, helping in the capture of Bristol and Exeter. In 1645, however, Cromwell's well trained forces moved westward and, when Pendennis Castle and St Michael's Mount surrendered after long sieges, the Royalist cause in Cornwall was lost.

Although Cornwall retained its individuality, by the end of the 16th century English had largely replaced Cornish as the spoken language. The last Cornish speaker is supposed to have been Dolly Pentreath who died in 1778; there is a monument to her in the church at Paul near Mousehole (see p.52).

The Cornish were still capable of asserting themselves, however, and in 1688 marched on Bristol when Jonathan Trelawny, Bishop of Winchester, was put in the Tower with five other bishops for opposing James II. They sang the song which had been sung 60 years earlier when Jonathan's grandfather had also been sent to the Tower:

And shall Trelawny die?
Then twenty thousand Cornishmen
will know the reason why

With King William III on the throne, Britain seemed to be set for quieter times. Cornwall had a flourishing fishing industry but from 1700 onwards it was in mining that the biggest development took place.

It was not tin, with which we always associate Cornwall, but copper that began to take first place. Shaft after shaft was sunk to extract the ore, and, by the mid-18th century, Cornwall was the largest supplier in the world. The ore was sent to south Wales for smelting. Steam power was harnessed for pumping the mines and engine houses dotted the Cornish landscape, particularly in the Land's End and Redruth areas. Cornwall became famous for her scientists such as Sir Humphry Davy, and engineers like Trevithick, credited with building the first steam locomotive for carrying passengers.

Although mining provided employment, conditions in the mines and in the homes were brutal, making for hard and drunken men. Poverty was rife, and the stories of smuggling and wrecking during this period should be seen against this background. A remarkable phenomenon of the time was the success of the campaign in Cornwall of John Wesley and his Methodists who, by their tireless preaching and devotion over many years, brought light and hope to hundreds. The chapels, to be found in even the tiniest of hamlets, testify to the impact Wesley made on Cornish life.

The dozens of derelict engine and boiler houses of the Cornish mines are a familiar picture. The story of the mines from the 1870s onwards is one of success and disaster. The copper boom lasted to about 1870. With new and cheaper sources being discovered in Australia, Africa, and the Americas, the bottom dropped out of the market. Hundreds of Cornish miners, the most skilful in the world, emigrated to avoid starvation and became the experts in running mines overseas.

There was a brief tin revival from 1870–72, but, by the 1890s, most of Cornwall's mines had been abandoned, never to work again. A few survived and were worked in the 1914–18 War but although money has been poured into many projects, the mining industry in Cornwall is as good as dead. At Pool near Redruth, by the A30, you can visit one of the famous beam engines which has been preserved.

Cornwall's other traditional industry suffered a severe blow at about the same time: the pilchard shoals which provided a livelihood for so many fishing villages disappeared from the coastal waters. No longer were the 'huers' on the cliffs able to signal by their shouts the approach of the red shoals. There were still mackerel and other fish but there were no longer salted pilchards to send abroad in quantities. Cornish fishing has never fully recovered.

In the latter half of the 19th century, the bleak outlook for Cornwall was transformed by the arrival of the railway. Fish, early vegetables and flowers were taken speedily to London and other centres. In the summer, Victorian holiday-makers began to discover the attractions of Cornwall's magnificent coastline and laid the foundations of the present thriving tourist trade.

In east Cornwall the china-clay industry flourishes. Before the mid-1700s, China was the only known source of china-clay. In about 1740 it was found in Limoges and Virginia. An obscure Devon chemist, William Cookworthy, encouraged by these discoveries, made some searches on his own and in 1746 found deposits at Tregonning near Porthleven (see p.55). He took out a patent in 1768 but derived no benefit from it. At first the clay was exploited by pottery firms from the Midlands, using disused tin workings, but is now used for many purposes from paper-making to face powder. The clay is extracted from the quartz by powerful jets of water, the huge white mounds of quartz waste dominating the landscape in the St Austell area. The methods used now are more mechanised and clay has become one of Britain's most valuable assets.

5 PENZANCE AND FALMOUTH

Penzance: (pop. 20,000) — the name Pens Sans, meaning holy headland, comes from the ancient chapel that stood above the harbour. In 1332 under Edward III, Penzance was granted a charter to hold fairs and markets and, thanks to its sheltered harbour and local trade, grew steadily, gaining borough status in 1614. Like most Cornish coastal towns, it was raided from the sea from time to time: in 1595 four Spanish ships landed 200 soldiers who sacked the town before Drake drove them away. Penzance much benefited by becoming an official 'coinage' town in 1663 (see p.11) for the assaying of tin from the mines of west Cornwall. The town was heavily engaged in smuggling in the 18th century. The famous chemist and inventor of the safety lamp, Sir Humphrey Davy, was born in Market Jew Street in 1778.

Penzance is a busy and attractive town: visit the Morrab Gardens and the Penlee Memorial Park with its Museum and 1,000-year-old Cornish Cross with a Latin inscription. The fascinating Geological Museum is in Alverton Street. There are 27 pubs to choose from. The Scilly Isles steamer service leaves from New Pier and the Heliport is just east of the town. The Castle Horneck Youth Hostel is 1 mile

(1½km) north-west of the centre.

The main street where the banks, etc, are situated is Alverton Street which continues eastwards into Market Jew Street.

Useful addresses
Information Office: Station Road (near the harbour)
Bus Station: Station Road (near the harbour)
Railway station: Station Road (near the harbour)
Youth Hostel: Castle Horneck
General Post Office: Market Jew Street
Police station: Penalverne Drive, off Alverton Street. Tel. 2395

Falmouth: (pop. 18,000) owes its creation to Sir John Killigrew, of a well known local family, who, at the end of the 16th century, urged the construction of a deep-water harbour on the site of two hamlets: Smith Hike and Penny-Come-Quick (Pen y cum gewic — headland by the valley of the creek). This was taken up and a quay built in 1660. In 1668 the legendary Falmouth Packets — small, fast vessels, lightly armed — started their regular mail services to the Americas and the West Indies. Later, Falmouth was the chosen port for ships of many nations to call 'for further orders'. On occasion, up to 300 ships could be seen anchored in the roadstead.

The docks were extended in the 19th century and, with the coming of the railway, Falmouth not only remained a busy port but became a favourite resort and yachting centre with its four beaches: Gyllynvase, Swanpool, Castle and Maen Porth. Along the waterfront is a most enjoyable walk: Church Street with its old shops, the Customs House — built by Sir Peter Killigrew — and Arwenack House, former home of the Killigrews.

Pendennis (castle headland) Castle was built as a harbour defence in 1544–6 by Henry VIII at the same time as St Mawes Castle on the other side of the estuary, during a period when invasion from France was expected. It can be visited: summer 9.30am-7pm; winter 10am-4.30pm. There is a Youth Hostel in the Castle. To get to the Castle, follow Castle Drive from the waterfront or from Cliff Road.

The Coast Path continues officially from Place which involves the crossing of two estuaries (see p.65).

The ferries to St Mawes and Flushing leave from the Prince of Wales Pier. There is no Sunday service November–March.

Useful addresses

Information and Accommodation Office: 28, Killigrew Street (centre of town)

Bus station: Berkeley Vale (centre of town)

Railway station: Avenue Road (near the Inner Harbour)

St Mawes Ferry: Prince of Wales Pier, Inner Harbour

Youth Hostel: Pendennis Castle

General Post Office: The Moor (centre of town)

Police station: Berkeley Vale. Tel. 312821

6 WILDLIFE

The abundance of wildlife on the Cornish coast will often bring you pleasant surprises as you walk.

One favourite is the grey seal, the only species of seal to be seen off the Cornish coast. Good vantage points to see them sunning themselves are off the Carracks, 3 miles (5km) west of St Ives (see p.44), and Stackhouse Cove, near Perranuthnoe (see p.54). The playful bottle-nosed dolphin and the common dolphin may be spotted from the cliff Path. You may also glimpse a pilot whale.

Commoner land mammals to be found in most parts of England are also found in Cornwall and may be encountered when you walk the Path. These include fox, hedgehog, rabbit — and, more locally, hare, stoat and weasel. In the woods, you may see grey squirrels or the occasional badger. The water vole may be seen in streams and, if you are very fortunate, there may be a glimpse of an otter in one of the bays or estuaries. The mink, from North America, is now quite common and even hunts on the sea shore. In the extensive woods just inland from the Path — the upper reaches of the Fal, for example — you may see a fallow deer.

Small mammals include field and harvest mice, field voles and three species of shrew, including the water shrew. These timid animals will take shelter rapidly when the walker's footsteps are detected but may be seen during 'sandwich stops'.

Reptiles, such as the adder, grass snake, slow worm and common lizard, are also likely to dash for cover at sounds of approach but can sometimes be seen sunning themselves. The adder, our only poisonous snake, can be identified by the dark zig-zag markings on its back. It can be found mainly in low-growing vegetation on cliff and moorland. One should not stray from the path if only wearing sandals, for example. The effect of an adder bite can be severe for children or invalids. Short-term ligature of the limb above the wound and sucking poison from the wound can be of immediate help before consulting a doctor.

Butterflies seen as you walk are likely to be of the commoner species: large white, speckled wood, small tortoiseshell, peacock, red admiral and orange-tipped as well as various kinds of blue butterfly. The brimstone could be seen as early as March. The famous large orange-and-black monarch or milkweed butterfly is a rare and distinguished visitor which has, on occasion, been seen — having been blown 3,000 miles (5,000km) off its normal migration course between North America and its winter home in the Mexican mountain forests!

Cornwall has been known over the centuries for its fishing grounds and the many varieties yield exciting catches. You may see a giant but harmless basking-shark cruising off Cornish shores, especially in mid-summer, feeding on plankton. The marine life of Cornwall's beaches is as varied as its type of shore. The observant visitor who enjoys beach-combing may be rewarded by finding other 'visitors': seeds and creatures that have drifted here from as far as the West Indies.

Birds

Bird-life is a constant source of interest as you walk along the Path. Some experience of bird identification is advantageous but even those with a limited knowledge have a good chance of observing rare species and their habits. You need field-glasses, a good bird book and a notebook to record on the spot what you see. You may be lucky enough to see a rarity. Care should be taken not to disturb the birds, especially during the nesting and breeding season.

The best times for birds in the area are during spring, autumn and winter. The spring and autumn are good times for walking the Path because of the abundance of birds, the mild weather and the relatively fewer numbers of tourists. The weather can also be surprisingly good for the keen observer of wintering birds.

According to the time of year and terrain, the Coast Path crosses areas popular with many different bird species. The following list gives the most common birds to look out for. In the list there is some inevitable overlap, both in habitat and season. The birds listed live on the Cornish coast throughout the year unless otherwise indicated: S=spring, SU=summer, A=autumn, W=winter. The breeding season is April–June.

Cliff-face: herring gull, great black-backed and occasionally lesser black-backed gull, fulmar, kittiwake, jackdaw, carrion crow, raven.

Sea-shore and rock: herring gull, great black-backed gull, black-headed gull (W), common gull (W), shag, cormorant, sandwich tern (SA), oyster-catcher, dunlin (W), curlew (W), rock pipit, pied wagtail, heron, turnstone (SAW), purple sandpiper (W), redshank (W), sanderling (W), ringed plover (W).

Cliff-top: wren, robin, stonechat, whitethroat (SU), kestrel, linnet, buzzard, chaffinch, goldfinch, dunnock, blackbird, willow warbler (SU), green woodpecker, grasshopper warbler (SU), wheatear (SU), cuckoo (SU).

Open field: skylark, yellowhammer, corn bunting, lapwing (W), fieldfare (W), redwing (W), swallow (SU), house-martin (SU), swift (SU), meadow pipit (SU), kestrel, buzzard.

Estuaries: redshank (W), herring gull, great black-backed gull (W), common gull (W), black-headed gull (W), greenshank (W), wigeon (W), golden and grey plover (W), mute swan, curlew, razorbill, guillemot (SU), black-tailed and bar-tailed godwit (W). Also wintering: divers, grebes, ringed plover, dunlin, red-breasted merganser.

Marsh and freshwater pools: mallard, teal, gadwall (W), shoveler (W), tufted duck (W), pochard (W), mute swan, moorhen, coot, Slavonian grebe (W), reed warbler (SU), sedge warbler (SU), heron, little grebe, water rail (W), dunlin (W), ringed plover (W). Also in passage: black tern, wood and green sandpiper, little stint.

Woodland and streams: song thrush, blackbird, green and great spotted woodpecker, great tit, blue tit, coal tit, nuthatch, tree creeper, goldcrest, jay, magpie, cuckoo (SU), chiffchaff (SU), sparrowhawk, tawny and barn owl, moorhen, coot, grey wagtail, spotted flychatcher (SU), kingfisher, pied wagtail, willow warbler.

Less common visitors which may also be seen in Cornwall on passage:

Spring: red kite, black kite, redstart, whinchat, ring ouzel, garganey, hoopoe, golden oriole.

Autumn: pied flycatcher, curlew, sandpiper, black redstart (some winter), firecrest, warblers, osprey.

Winter: predators include hen-harrier, peregrine, merlin, and short-eared owl. Divers — great northern, black-throated, red-throated. Eider, scoter, and mergansers may also be found and look out for rare gulls in winter e.g. glaucous, Iceland and Mediterranean.

In spring and autumn many rare birds turn up e.g. egret, spoonbill, waders, and rare passerines.

Areas of particular interest

Section numbers in brackets.

Camel Estuary (12) Winter divers (near mouth of estuary): great northern, black-throated, red-throated; great-and lesser black-backed gull, black-headed and common gull, golden plover, knot, mallard, teal, wigeon, shelduck, shoveler, goldeneye, dunlin, black and bar-tailed godwit, white-fronted goose.

Autumn (mainly): migrating terns, herring gull, oyster catcher, common sand-piper, redshank, shelduck. Occasional: osprey, peregrine falcon. Large heronry on the south bank.

Helford and Falmouth (45,46) Rivers and creeks. Passage and wintering: redshank and spotted redshank, greenshank, common and green sandpiper, dunlin, divers and grebes.

Hayle Estuary (24) herring and great and lesser black-backed gull, golden plover, dunlin, teal, wigeon, goldeneye, lapwing, great northern diver, knot.

Land's End (31) Cliff or islands: herring, great and lesser black-backed gulls, kittiwake, fulmar.

Migrants: swallow, swift, sand-martin, house-martin, warblers.

Passage: guillemot, razorbill, shearwater, kittiwake, skua, tern, gannet, puffin, sea ducks.

Breeding: kestrel, wheatear, buzzard, stonechat, cuckoo, meadow-pipit.

Lizard (41) Arrival and departure of migrants as at Land's End. Equally good observation post. Flocks of wintering skylarks, chaffinches, fieldfares, redwings.

Loe Pool (38) Wintering ducks: mallard, teal, gadwall, shoveler, tufted duck, pochard. Also mute swan, heron, moorhen, coot. Summer: reed and sedge warbler. Winter: dabchick.

Lye Rock (7) Cliff nesting in breeding season: herring and great black-backed gull, fulmar, razorbill, guillemot, shag, cormorant.

Marazion Marsh (35) Heronry; reed and sedge warblers in summer. Important as a migration stop for birds, particularly waterfowl and wading birds. Wintering waterfowl.

Mullion Island (39) Nature Reserve. Breeding: great black-backed gull, razorbill, kittiwake, fulmar, cormorant, shag.

St Ives Island (25) Good observation post for migrating birds on passage in autumn: gannet, Manx shearwater, great and arctic skua, common, arctic and sandwich terns, fulmar, kittiwake, grebes, divers and sea ducks.

The Cornwall Birdwatching and Preservation Society is a vigorous organisation whose many members keep a close watch on every species found in Cornwall and the Scillies. Their annual reports to members contain accounts of breeding, migrant and passage species, with fascinating photographs and notes. Details of the Society should be available at all Cornish Public Libraries.

For information about all forms of Cornish wildlife, the Cornish Biological Records Unit at Pool, near Camborne, can recommend a wide range of books. Their unique archive has over 1 million records of some 25,000 species. The address is: Trevithick Building, Trevenson Road, Pool, Redruth. Tel (01203) 710424. Open weekdays. Visitors welcome.

7 FLOWERS AND PLANTS

The Cornish Coast Path passes over various types of terrain, with the flora displaying a similar diversity. The high exposed heath, with typical flora, of Land's End changes almost at once to the warm sheltered coves of Lamorna and Porthcurno. Sub-tropical plants thrive in the Morrab Gardens of Penzance. The Lizard Nature Reserve, covering 244 acres (98¾ hectares) contains a number of rarities and, in common with the gentler but wild slopes between Fowey and Polperro, is of great botanical interest. The purpose of these notes is to give to those who already know something about the subject an idea of some of the species likely to be seen.

Woodland: coppice oak, both sessile and common oaks. Elm thickets including the small-leaved Cornish elm. Introduced sycamore and ash. Monterey pine grows well in exposed places. Typical flowers: bluebell, lesser celandine, wood sorrel, wood avens, common cow wheat, bilberry (locally called 'urts), golden saxifrage, Cornish moneywort and, rarely, bastard balm. A splendid fern population includes hay-scented buckler fern, royal fern, hard fern, Tunbridge filmy fern, hart's tongue, golden scale male fern and lady fern. Stands of introduced turkey and holm oaks withstand the salt air well.

Coastal scrub: locally developed in small valleys and disturbed ground areas. Common species include tamarisk, wild privet, sycamore, European gorse, blackthorn, elder and brambles. Ground flora very restricted in these places.

Dry heathland: dominated by western gorse and bell heather with ling, tormentil, sawwort, betony, madder, dodder, leafy hawkweed and a variety of mosses and lichens including Cladonia. Ling-dominated areas are often more exposed to the sea and have maritime species including thrift, sea and buck's horn plantain, sea carrot, vernal squill, and centaury, also locally prostrate broom. Other species include bird's foot trefoil, wild thyme, slender-flowered thistle, English stonecrop, carline thistle and sheep's bit. Grass-dominated sward of sheep's fescue and bristle bent grasses with scurvy grass, thrift, bluebell and primroses.

Wet heathland: locally bog moss areas with pale butterwort, round and long-leaved sundews, devil's bit scabious, bog pimpernel. Purple moor grass areas with bog rush and royal fern, also purple loosestrife, and cotton grasses.

Rock Flora: natural cliff outcrops: thrift, common and golden samphire, rock sea spurry, sea beet, sea spleenwort, rock sea lavender, common scurvy grass and early scurvy grass, sea and buck's horn plaintain, sea mayweed, sea campion, yellow stonecrop, English stonecrop, wild thyme, penny wort. Mine heaps: ling, western and European gorse, tormentil, thrift foxglove, weld, ragwort, southern marsh orchid.

Dunes: marram and sea lyme grass and a wide variety of other lime-suited species. Beaked hawk's beard, carline thistle, cowslip, hound's tongue, kidney vetch, ploughman's spikenard, rest harrow, salad burnet, spotted cat's ear, stinking iris, vipers bugloss, wild carrot, yellow wort, stork's bill.

Arable and pasture, some rough: ragwort, birds foot trefoil, coltsfoot, mouse-ear chickweed, primrose, winter heliotrope, alexanders, wild teasel, sea mayweed, yellow bartsia, three-cornered leek, yellow rattle, pale flax, rest harrow, foxglove, hairy tare, corn spurrey, common fumitory, corn marigold, red valerian, hogweed and common cat's ear.

8 GEOLOGY

These short notes on the geology of the coast of Cornwall are not designed for the expert but simply to draw attention to general elementary geological features which may be of interest.

As with the rest of the South-West Peninsula, the greater part of the rock structure is of sedimentary origin i.e. formed from beds of rock that were laid down hundreds of millions of years ago on the sea bed or on the beds of lakes. They can be described generally as mudstones, sandstones and limestones. Immense geological pressures have sometimes bent the strata into the strange shapes to be seen in the cliffs at Millook Haven (see p.22) or the bands of limestone and sandstone on the beach at Bude (see p.21). The Land's End Peninsula, Bodmin Moor, and the Redruth and St Austell areas are composed, however, of granite which not only gives us the awe-inspiring cliffs of Land's End and the rather bare uplands of north Cornwall, but was also the chief factor in the geological origins of the mineral wealth of the area and the former flourishing mining industry — mainly tin and copper ore.

Granite is an igneous rock — one which has been thrust up in a molten state into the generally older local sedimentary beds, cooling and hardening slowly, sometimes close to the surface. It has subsequently been eroded by such forces as the weather and sea, leaving exposed huge 'bosses' of which Land's End, Bodmin Moor and Dartmoor are examples. One difference between sedimentary and igneous types is that sedimentary strata are fossil-bearing; no fossils are found in igneous rock. The cooling molten granite had the effect, through immense pressures and heat, of radically changing the sedimentary rock with which it came into contact, forming liquids and gases that eventually solidified as mineral ores.

Farther round the coast between Falmouth and St Austell, in the Portholland area, another strip of igneous rock called gabbro is quarried, the stone being widely used for road making. Nare Head is an instance where the igneous rock, greenstone, has proved more resistant to the sea and weather, forming a promontory.

The geology of the area is a vital factor in archaeological research. Neolithic Man made his chamber tombs and entrance graves from the hard granite he found around him. This is one reason why we have more Neolithic remains in the Land's End Peninsula than in the whole of the rest of the south-west.

Raised beaches are common around the south coast in particular. There are also submerged forests representing ancient woodlands overwhelmed by the sea level rising within the last few thousand years, and possibly accounting for the legends of the lost land of Lyonesse. One such forest lies off Mount's Bay.

The areas which have been subject to geological changes are called metamorphic aureoles i.e. 'rings' or 'halos' round the edge of the granite (in this case). This is the reason why, as soon as you start walking on the Path westwards from St Ives, you come upon traces of the now almost defunct mining industry. The coastal strip near Land's End, as well as other Cornish areas such as Redruth and St Agnes, are situated on a 'metamorphic aureole' and this is where the ores of copper, tin and other metals such as silver and gold were found and exploited. The Celts of 3,000 years ago were 'streaming' the tin from the rivers, and this was the method used in Roman times and in the Middle Ages. From the 18th century onwards, mine shafts were dug to hack out the ore-bearing rock in greater quantities.

After the mining industry declined, mainly because of overseas competition (see p.12), another Cornish industry developed, originating from the granite areas of the county. This is the china clay industry, which straddles the Coast Path near Par, and produces the unsightly mountains of white waste in the hinterland. China-clay is actually granite, which has decomposed over millions of years by the action of water originating deep in the earth's crust.

Section 1
MARSLAND MOUTH-
STANBURY MOUTH
2 miles (3¼km); strenuous

The north Cornish Coast Path starts at Marsland Mouth, the Devon/Cornwall border. The nearest access by road is at Welcombe Mouth (Devon), ½ mile (¾km) by steep path to the north. For access road, turn off the A39 at Welcombe Cross which is 2 miles (3¼km) from Welcombe Mouth. Other Devon access points on the Path nearby are Hartland Quay, which is 2½ miles (4km) from the border; Hartland Point which is 5½ miles (8¾km) from the border and Clovelly 13½ miles (21¾km) from the border.

Between Marsland Mouth and Stanbury Mouth you have no less than four steep-sided combes to cross which makes this scenically rewarding section hard work and should not be attempted by inexperienced walkers.

Note the twisted strata of Gull Rock just off the coast.

From the top of Marsland Cliff, the Path crosses two deep combes before reaching Henna Cliff from where, looking inland, the church and village of Morwenstow are visible.

A short way down the slope, the footpath turns inland from the Coast Path to woods and the vicarage, home of the 19th-century Cornish poet and eccentric parson, the Reverend R.S. Hawker, said to have introduced the Harvest Festival. A great rescuer of shipwrecked crews, he forbad looting. Many seafarers are buried in the churchyard.

Turn back to the Coast Path by the footpath from the church up the slope of the valley and you come to a National Trust sign. A few yards down the cliff, you will come to the hut built by Hawker from driftwood, in which he would write in splendid solitude.

Climb up to the viewpoint on Higher Sharpnose Point and then the exposed ridge path descends sharply to the stream at Stanbury Mouth and up the other side.

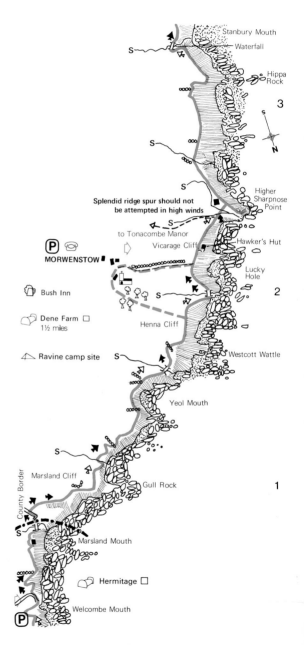

Section 2
STANBURY MOUTH–
NORTHCOTT MOUTH

3½ miles (5½km); strenuous
Cum. 5½ miles (8¾km)

Once at the bottom of the wide valley at Stanbury Mouth, also accessible by a farm track, the Path up the opposite side continues over rough heathland, past the tracking station, through the area of the former army camp, past a disused Coast Guard look-out, and finally, close to the cliff edge, to Coombe Valley. From Steeple Point you drop down to the popular sandy Duckpool Beach. No facilities apart from a car park.

From Steeple Point looking inland is Coombe Valley, owned by the National Trust. The farm above the valley to the south is Stowe Barton (Barton meaning farmstead). The stables are all that remain of the grand 17th-century home of the Grenville family. Nearby was Stowe, home of Sir Richard Grenville, the West Country Elizabethan hero who accompanied Raleigh's first expedition to Virginia in 1585 and whose career is so vividly described in A.L. Rowse's *Sir Richard Grenville of the* Revenge.

The Path continues, over Stowe Cliff, before descending to Sandy Mouth, another popular beach, with refreshment booth and car park. From Sandy Mouth the going is less precipitous and in half an hour you are at Northcott Mouth where there are refreshments available and the beach is a fine wide stretch of sand.

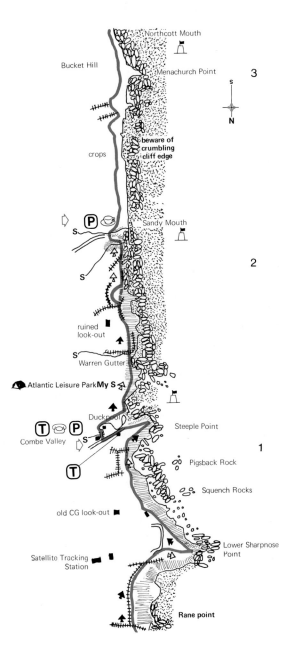

Section 3
NORTHCOTT MOUTH–BUDE–
HIGHER LONGBEAK
4 miles (6½km); easy
Cum. 9½ miles (15¼km)

From Northcott Mouth it is a mile (1½km) to Bude. You can either walk along the cliffs or the sands below. Take care as the sands become covered at high tide (see p.6 for tides).

Bude (pop. 5,700) is a small resort town and surfing centre. It is joined to Stratton with its Norman church and old pub, The Tree. The Tree was the Royalist headquarters in 1643 during the battle of Stamford Hill above Stratton, won by the Cavaliers under Sir Bevil Grenville, who was a descendent of the famous Sir Richard. A hero of the occasion was Anthony Payne, a Cornish giant, who lived at The Tree.

The Bude Canal was built in 1823 to transport sand to Holsworthy but now only 2 miles (3¼km) are navigable. The castle, now council offices, was built in 1830 by Sir Goldsworthy Gurney, a Cornish inventor. From Bude southwards, there are rock outcrops of all shapes and sizes, resulting from the action of weather and sea working along the softer shale outcrops, leaving the more resistant sandstone and local limestone bands upstanding.

For the Coast Path at Bude, follow the road across the river and the canal and up Church Path. The Path will be seen leading up to the tower on the cliff. At low tide, it is possible to cross the river by a little bridge nearer the sea. A pleasant walk follows the cliff over Efford Down until the road with its houses almost crowds the Path off the scene. You have to bear with this for 1½ miles (2½km) until you come to Widemouth Sand.

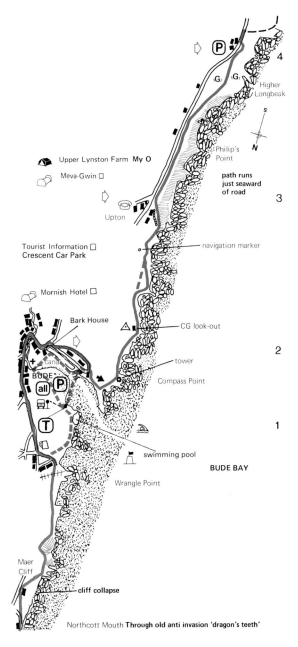

Higher Longbeak

Philip's Point

path runs just seaward of road

Upper Lynston Farm

Meva-Gwin

Upton

navigation marker

Tourist Information
Crescent Car Park

Mornish Hotel

Bark House

CG look-out

tower

Compass Point

BUDE
all

swimming pool

BUDE BAY

Wrangle Point

Maer Cliff

cliff collapse

Northcott Mouth **Through old anti invasion 'dragon's teeth'**

Section 4
WIDEMOUTH SAND-
BYNORTH CLIFF
3½ miles (5½km); moderate
Cum. 13 miles (21km)

The Path continues along the low cliff above the broad sands of Widemouth Bay past the old Salthouse cottage or you can walk along the sands. At Wanson Mouth, the Path takes to the road for a short distance and then begins to climb. Soon the caravans and bungalows of Widemouth are out of sight. The scene becomes wilder with fine views of cliff and sea, descending eventually to the small bay at Millook Haven which is a private beach.

The cliff which you have just come down is much photographed for the extraordinary zig-zag formations of the rock strata, shales and sandstone which can be seen from the road at the Haven.

Follow the road which climbs steeply out of Millook Haven. At the top of the rise you will see the Path on the right of the road. From here the route lies along the cliff-top pastures and across a wooded combe cut by a small stream.

The wood of stunted sessile oaks is of interest as it is the only one in Cornwall to survive the coastal gales and the extensive felling for bark for use in tanning.

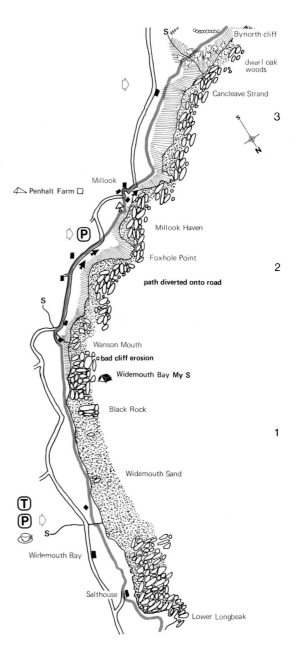

Section 5
DIZZARD POINT–
NORTHERN DOOR ARCH
4¼ miles (6¾km); strenuous
Cum. 17¼ miles (27¾km)

You walk along the edge of rough pastureland for some time without sighting any human habitation. You cross three steep-sided combes, the last one bringing you above Pencannow Point. After rounding the 400-foot (120m) headland, a track runs diagonally straight down the hillside into Crackington Haven.

The huge 430-foot (130m) cliffs, with their strangely contorted rock strata, tower above the small collection of houses, village stores and pub — the Coombe Barton — which compose Crackington Haven. The church of St Gennys, of 11th-century foundation, lies in an idyllic situation at the end of a lane 1 mile (1½km) away, and is worth a visit. Crackington Beach is suitable for surfing.

From the beach, the route of the Path is clear, running over the gorse-covered cliff fringing the south shore until, climbing gradually, the sharp headland, Cambeak, is rounded. Below, a little farther on is a large rock arch known as Northern Door, and then the menacing Samphire Rock which juts out on the beach.

The National Trust owns most of the 3 miles (5km) of coast from Cleave Strand to beyond the Northern Door, most of it a magnificent gift in memory of an aircrew lost during World War II.

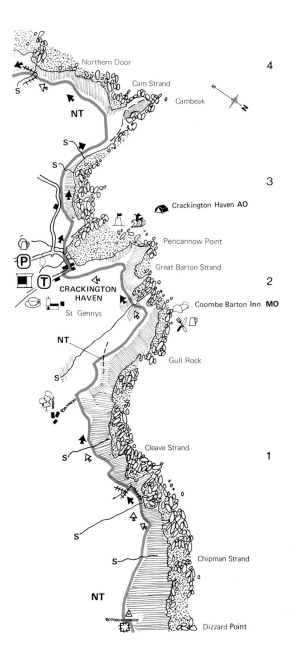

Northern Door

Cam Strand

Cambeak

NT

Crackington Haven AO

Pencannow Point

Great Barton Strand

CRACKINGTON
HAVEN

St Gennys

Coombe Barton Inn MO

NT

Gull Rock

Cleave Strand

Chipman Strand

NT

Dizzard Point

Section 6

SAMPHIRE ROCK–BOSCASTLE

4¼ miles (6¾km); strenuous

Cum. 21½ miles (34½km)

There is fine cliff-walking on this stretch with quite steep climbs in the first 2 miles (3¼km). From the cliff-top above the Samphire Rock, you have a good view of the boulder-strewn beach known as the Strangles, with its wild region of scrub between the cliff edge and the sea.

It is believed that Thomas Hardy based a scene in his early novel *A Pair of Blue Eyes* on the Strangles. It was familiar to him when, as a young man working for a Dorchester architect, he was engaged in restoring the church of St Juliot near Boscastle. It was here that he fell in love with the rector's sister-in-law, Emma Gifford, who became his first wife. There are paths down to the beach from the cliff. At Trevigue Farm just off the Path there is a National Trust Information Centre. Accommodation, meals and refreshments are provided in the summer season.

The Path then begins the ascent of High Cliff which rises 731 feet (223m). From the choice of paths, keep to the highest on the hillside. There is a sharp drop on the other side through the rough ground of Rusey Cliff, the south boundary of National Trust land.

The Path continues along the edge of pastureland for about 1½ miles (2½km) before the slope down to Pentargon where the small stream empties onto the beach in a spectacular 120-foot (37m) waterfall. After the climb out of the little valley, the route follows a wall on the seaward side. You then come round Penally Hill with its prominent weather vane.

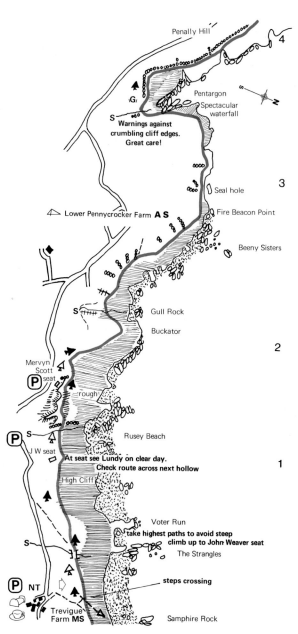

Penally Hill

4

G

Pentargon

Spectacular waterfall

S

Warnings against crumbling cliff edges. Great care!

3

Seal hole

Lower Pennycrocker Farm **A S**

Fire Beacon Point

Beeny Sisters

S

Gull Rock

Buckator

2

Mervyn Scott

P seat

rough

Rusey Beach

P S

J W seat

At seat see Lundy on clear day. Check route across next hollow

1

High Cliff

Voter Run

take highest paths to avoid steep climb up to John Weaver seat

S

The Strangles

steps crossing

P NT

Trevigue Farm **MS**

Samphire Rock

Section 7

BOSCASTLE–TINTAGEL

4½ miles (7¼km); moderate

Cum. 26 miles (41¾km)

The name Boscastle is derived from the Bottreaux family, mediaeval lords of the manor. The harbour was built by Sir Richard Grenville in Elizabeth I's reign. The village's lime-washed and thatched houses are a photographer's dream. There are three pubs: The Wellington, The Cobweb and The Napoleon which was used for recruiting in the Napoleonic Wars. On the quay are the National Trust information office and shop as well as the Youth Hostel. A footpath up the wooded Valency valley leads to the beautiful old Minster.

The Coast Path climbs from the south side of the harbour, round Willapark (meaning 'look-out') and continues along the cliff, past Forrabury Common, still cultivated in the Celtic strip system. Seaward of the Path, off the prominent arched rock called the Ladies Window, you can see Long Island and Short Island, breeding places for many sea-birds; as is Lye Rock, 1 mile (1½km) to the south (see Birds, p.16). Next is Rocky Valley, with an attractive footpath inland.

Up the Rocky Valley path, on a rock near a ruined mill are two circular 'maze'-type carvings about 9 inches across, possibly Bronze Age. Where a road crosses the stream is Trevillett Mill, which has been carefully restored. Refreshments are available. Continuing up the footpath on the other side of the road you for about ¾ mile (1¼km) you come to St Nectan's Kieve (kieve meaning 'tub'), an impressive waterfall and site of a 6th-century shrine. Allow 1 hour to St Nectan's Kieve and return. Look out for dippers in the stream.

The Path crosses the neck of the Willapark headland, site of an Iron Age cliff castle.

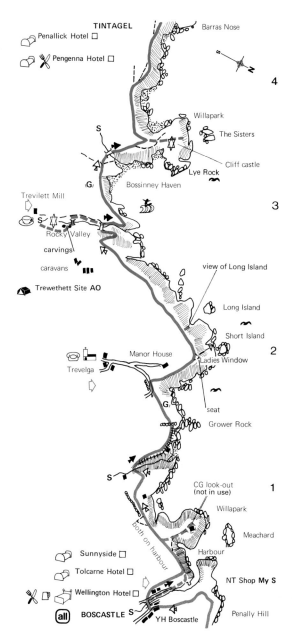

25

Section 8

TINTAGEL–
TREGONNICK TAIL

3¾ miles (6km); moderate
Cum. 29¾ miles (47¾km)

Tintagel owes much of its fame to the King Arthur legend as proclaimed by Tennyson in the last century. For those familiar with *Idylls of the King,* it can be quite moving to stand on the island and its tiny cove. The site is also important for the remains of England's earliest monastery, built by Celtic missionaries from Wales in *c.*AD500. They brought back the light of Christianity to a country enveloped in the ruin of the Dark Ages. The ruins of the 12th-century castle are also impressive: parts of the Great Hall are still standing. A booklet on the island is available. The only attraction of Tintagel village is the Old Post Office, formerly a 15th-century manor house.

The Coast Path climbs up south of the castle site.

Tintagel church of St Materiana, Norman with earlier parts, can be visited by a short detour.

Tintagel Youth Hostel, housed in former slate quarry offices, is at Dunderhole Point, from where there are excellent views. The Path continues, following the cliff edge. The pillar of rock at Hole Beach was left by quarrymen as a shelter. Trebarwith Strand (Port William) formerly shipped slate. There are sands at low tide and the Strand is suitable for surfing. The pub is The Port William.

The Mill House pub is ½ a mile (¾km) inland.

The Path leads off the drive of The Port William pub, then up the hill. Descend down to the bridge over the stream at Backways Cove and then up the steep south side through the gorse parallel to the cliff.

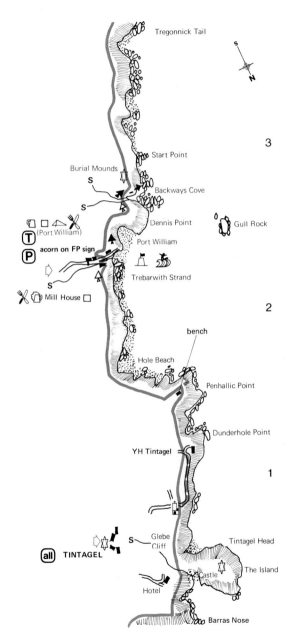

Section 9

TREGARDOCK BEACH–
PORT GAVERNE

4 miles (6½km); strenuous
Cum. 33¾ miles (54¼km)

The Path here crosses a wild and unspoiled stretch with some steep combes to negotiate. At first, it continues round the seaward end of a fence and then, in the narrow space available along the cliff edge, to the headland, Tregonnick Tail, above Tregardock Beach, which is a tumbled break in the cliffs. The beach is dominated by a large hump — The Mountain — round which the Path winds.

Tregardock Cliff is National Trust land, with access from a farm off the B3314 road by footpath. There is a sandy beach for a few hours at low water. Swimming and surfing should be reserved for the experts.

Once past Tregardock, the Path drops steeply down to the bottom of a little combe. Then you proceed up the other side and, keeping close to the cliff edge for some distance, you pass a disused Coast Guard look-out (keep seaward of the fence) and descend to a wide valley.

On the south side of the next valley there appears to be a cave entrance. It is actually the entrance to a tunnel — now unusable — leading down to the next beach, Barrett's Zawn (zawn meaning 'chasm'), through which slate was drawn from a beach quarry.

Go round the spectacular Barrett's Zawn and then follow the Path down another steep little valley, the banks of which in Spring are covered by primroses. Continue along Bound's Cliff and the Path drops down to Port Gaverne and the Port Gaverne Hotel.

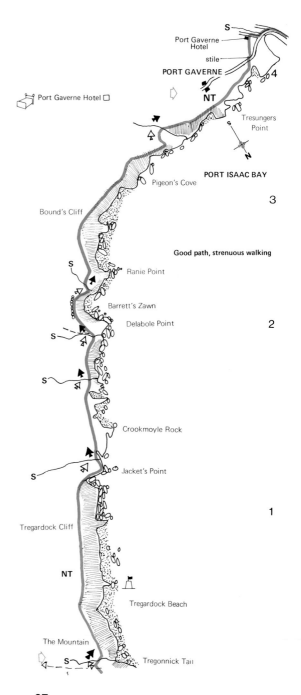

Section 10
PORT GAVERNE–PORT ISAAC–LUNDY BAY

4½ miles (7¼km); strenuous
Cum. 38¼ miles (61½km)

After ¼ mile (400m) from Port Gaverne, the Path turns off seaward, rounds the headland and continues down to Port Isaac.

Port Isaac (Cornish for 'corn port') is one of the most attractive Cornish villages. Its small 15th-century quay is no longer busy with fishing boats but, round the harbour, the old houses look much the same as in the past. The narrow streets and passages, one only 18 inches wide — 'Squeezibelly Alley' — are delightful.

Follow the Public Footpath sign standing at the foot of the narrow street which climbs out of the town on the south side of the harbour. From there, the Path rounds Lobber Point and then slopes down to the idyllic Pine Haven. Rising to the cliff top, it crosses the neck of Varley Head and continues its switchback way round Kellan Head to Port Quin, an excellent cliff walk.

Port Quin has a few cottages and a building once used for salting fish. Dwindling pilchard shoals were the probable cause of the desertion of the village in the 1840s. There are no shops or facilities for food in the village.

Take the road going south out of Port Quin. Near the top of the rise, the Path leads off seaward past a National Trust holiday house.

On Doyden Point is a 19th-century 'folly', Doyden Castle, used by the owner for gambling parties. It is now another National Trust house. By the next stile on the Path are the old shafts of a lead/silver mine which are fenced around.

The Path, with fine views, continues along the cliffs, all in the National Trust territory, bringing you to Lundy Bay, a fine sandy beach in quiet, green surroundings.

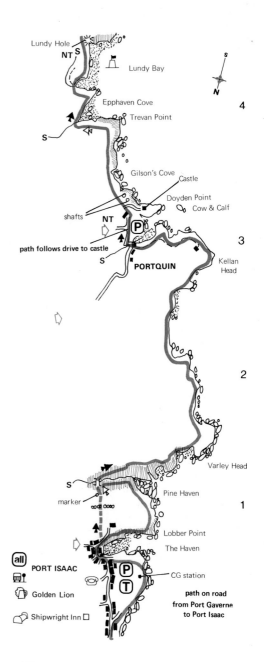

Section 11
PORT QUIN BAY–
NEW POLZEATH
3¾ miles (6km); easy
Cum. 42 miles (67½km)

This section provides fine walking with no problems. From Lundy Bay, the National Trust has signposted the Path clearly. Where the route branches, the sign directs you round Carnweather Point towards Rumps Point, climbing through the gorse above Port Quin Bay.

The landscape, coastal and inland, has changed. The cliffs are not so high and the countryside has become gentler and softer.

The cliff Path turns west above the headland of Rumps Point, well worth a detour.

The outline of the impressive Rumps Point cliff castle, a fortified settlement of the Iron Age or even earlier, can be seen to advantage from the Path. A triple rampart across the neck of the headland defended access; the position of the entrances can also be made out. Excavations have produced pottery from the 1st century BC to the 1st century AD.

On, round Pentire Head, follow the path high through sheep pasture.

The rock formation has changed. The sedimentary slates and shales have given way to igneous rocks, i.e. rocks that were once molten. The rocks at Pentire Point itself are mignificent 'pillow' lavas representing the fossilised outpourings of a once massive submarine volcano.

You now turn south-east and drop down to Pentireglaze Haven where there is a small sandy beach. The Path then climbs steeply for the short distance to the road above and the terrace of houses facing Hayle Bay in New Polzeath. The Atlantic Hotel, the only pub in the resort, occupies one of these houses.

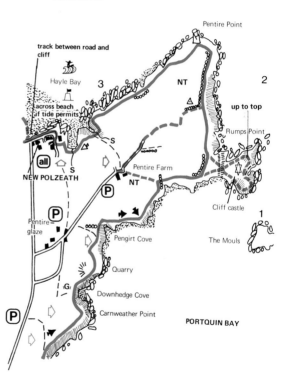

Section 12

NEW POLZEATH–PADSTOW–
STEPPER POINT

5½ miles (8¾km) plus ferry trip;
easy; Cum. 47½ miles (76½km)

A pleasant, quiet walk. From the terrace in New Polzeath, the Path leads down through the sandhills to Polzeath at the Bay's head, with fine sands and surfing. From the road running south, on the right, the Path runs between houses and along the fine turf promenade known as the Greenaway to Daymer Bay and its sandy beach. An interesting alternative is the path across the golf course marked by low white posts and posts with yellow arrows.

To the left of the Path is the early 15th-century church of St Enodoc on the site of a 6th-century oratory. For years it was buried by encroaching sands. Keep on the marked track, rejoining the official Path on the other side of Brae Hill.

The Path continues along the shore for ¾ mile (1km) to Rock. There is a ferry to Padstow: Apr.-Oct. daily; Nov.-Mar. weekdays (last boat: summer 7.30pm; winter 4.30pm). Departures are from near Westerly Sailing School. Car parking available.

Padstow (pop. 2,300), an attractive old fishing port, has been a borough since 1583. The church of St Petroc dates mainly from the 15th century. There are two very early Celtic crosses in the churchyard. Prideaux Place (1598) is still the family home. John Prideaux was on the expedition to Virginia with Grenville (see p.20). On May Day Hobby Horse Festival, a man dressed as a horse runs through the streets among singing crowds.

The Path leads from the harbour to North Quay, then along the estuary to Harbour Cove, an old lifeboat station. It then continues to the tower on Stepper Point.

The sandbank, the Doom Bar, visible at low tide, has wrecked hundreds of ships.

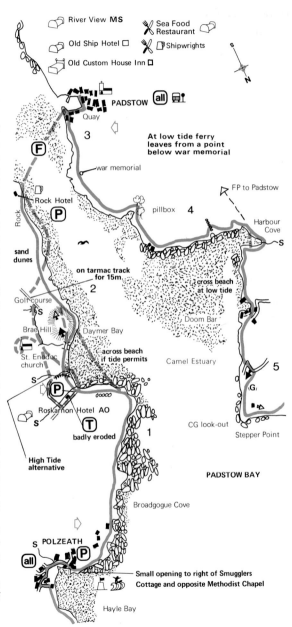

30

Section 13
PEPPER HOLE–TREVONE– HARLYN BAY
3¾ miles (6km); easy
Cum. 51¼ miles (82½km)

The Coast Path is clear from Stepper Point along the cliffs, with impressive rocky views. The route passes Porthmissen, a small promontory with an arch carved by the sea and then, just seaward of the Path, Round Hole, where the roof of a sea cave has collapsed.

Trevone is a small, popular resort with good sands. Few facilities, but there are two pubs at St Merryn 1¾ miles (3km) inland.

From Trevone, the Path keeps to the low coastline until the sandy, sheltered Harlyn Beach is reached.

There are only a few houses in Harlyn but it is known for archaeological discoveries made in the district. The most important discovery was in 1900 when an Iron Age cemetery with over 100 slate coffins was found containing, with human remains, a variety of bronze and iron ornaments. A number of the finds are exhibited in Truro Museum. Earlier at Harlyn, two beautiful Celtic gold lunulae (crescent-shaped ornaments) about 8 inches wide, of fine workmanship and about 3,000 years old, were found. These also can be seen in Truro Museum.

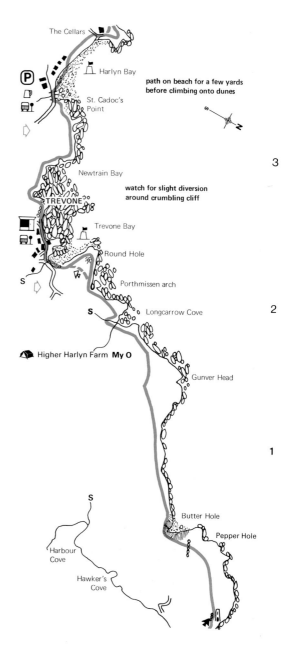

31

Section 14
POLVENTON BAY-
PORTHCOTHAN
5½ miles (8¾km); easy
Cum. 56¾ miles (91¼km)

Just over the bridge in Harlyn the Path leads up to Trevose Head from the sands of the beach, past some bungalows and, keeping close to the coastline, rounds Polventon (or Mother Ivey's) Bay. It passes a caravan site and Mother Ivey's Cottage en route. At the far end of the Bay is the Padstow Lifeboat Station.

Trevose Head, like other headlands in the area, is composed of rocks of volcanic origin, more resistant to the sea than the sedimentary local formations. The lighthouse can be visited on weekday afternoons. Fine views are to be had on a clear day of the whole north Cornish coast from St Ives to Hartland Point.

On turning south from Trevose Head, you drop down to Booby Bay and the adjacent wide Constantine Bay. Fine sands are exposed by the tide but bathing can be dangerous because of the rocks. The Path follows the dunes round the shore, or you can walk on the sands. Over a small rise you come to Treyarnon Bay where the surfing is good. Treyarnon Youth Hostel is right on the Bay, overlooking the sea. From Treyarnon Bay there is an easy ascent to the top of the cliffs which, although not very high, drop sheer. After a fine cliff-top walk of about a mile (1½km) you come to the fine beach at Porthcothan.

It was on these cliffs that the Cornish Chough (a red-legged bird of the crow family), the county's emblem, last bred. It is now found only in Wales and Scotland. There is one pub, The Treorea, at Porthcothan, and a place for teas in the season. Car parking is available and the bay is suitable for surfing.

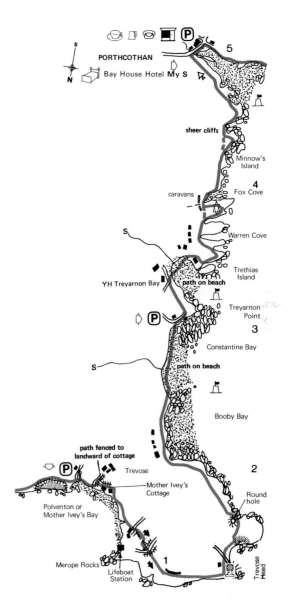

Section 15

PORTHCOTHAN-
MAWGAN PORTH

4½ miles (7¼km); moderate

Cum. 61¼ miles (98½km)

The Coast Path, with fine, straightforward cliff-top walking, leads up from the road at Porthcothan, along and above the south shore of the beach. Continuing past a few houses, it climbs gradually to Park Head. It is National Trust land most of the way.

After passing Park Head, a zig-zag path known as Pentire Steps leads down to the beach.

A short distance further on the Coastal Path and you come to the famous Bedruthan Steps, although owing to landslides access by the steps may be temporarily closed.

The Steps are rock islands of volcanic origin left isolated through erosion. There is a car park, National Trust shop, toilets and refreshments in season. As you approach Bedruthan, you will see Redcliffe Castle, an Iron Age promontory fort. This part of the coast was fatal for shipping before the Trevose Lighthouse was built in 1847. The brig *Samaritan*, with a cargo of cotton and silks was wrecked off the Steps in 1846 with only two survivors. For months afterwards, the locals were decked out in finery looted from the wreck. They heartlessly named it The Good Samaritan and one of the Steps is known as Samaritan Island.

Continuing from Bedruthan, the Path runs through rough gorse on the cliff-top down to Mawgan Porth, a bungalow resort with a good sandy beach and surfing. Over the bridge, the Path climbs steeply off the road to the right, towards Berryl's Point. The Merrymore is an old pub, frequented by fishermen.

Close to the main road in the village is the site of a small Dark Ages settlement and cemetery dating from *c.* AD500. Apply to beach café or garage to view.

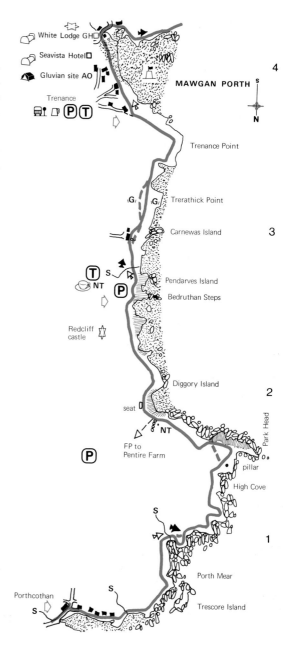

Section 16

BERRYL'S POINT–
NEWQUAY

4½ miles (7¼km); easy

Cum. 65¾ miles (105¾km)

From Berryl's Point, the Path rounds Beacon Cove — there is a steep path down to the beach — and then continues across the headland, Griffin's Point.

On Griffin's Point is another well-defined Iron Age fortification with two ramparts and ditches.

*There is now a 2-mile (3¼km) walk along the 200-foot (60m) cliffs above Watergate Beach. A gap in the cliff gives access to the beach, a favourite for surfers and there is a guest house with car parking. From here, you can continue along the cliff or, **at low tide only**, on the sands. Approaching Newquay you come to Trevelgue Head, a promontory half occupied by a putting-green.*

Here, at Trevelgue Head, is the most impressive cliff castle in Cornwall, with six ramparts and ditches, occupied from *c.* 2,000BC to Roman times.

Porth (or St Columb Porth), now part of Newquay, has a fine sandy beach at low tide. Follow the road round the beach , past Porth Bay Hotel, down the steps on the left at a bus shelter and under the road bridge. The Path then leads along the cliff above the beach, turning south to join Lusty Glaze Road and into Newquay.

Newquay (pop. 16,000). The name Newquay derives from the 'new quay' which the small fishing hamlet of Towan Blistra was authorised to build in 1439. Pilchard fishing was the mainstay of the town: the Huer's House above the harbour is where the 'huer' would spot the shoals and direct the fishermen. In the last century coal was imported for the tin mines. When this declined, the tourist trade took over. The five sandy beaches, now with surfing and supervised bathing, attract thousands.

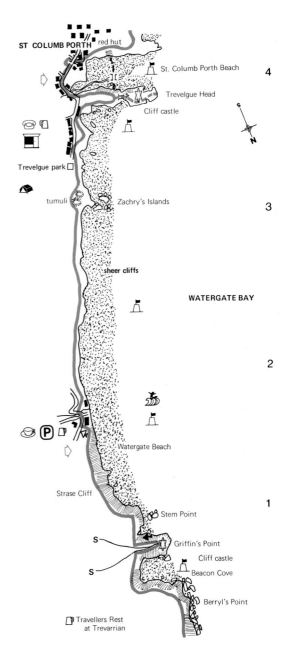

34

Section 17
FISTRAL BAY (NEWQUAY)–
HOLYWELL
5½ miles (8¾km); easy
Cum. 71¼ miles (114½km)

*To get to the Coast Path from the harbour in
Newquay, take the steps leading up from the
north side of the quay; this brings you out on
a road encircling a large hotel — the Huer's
House is on your right. The Path starts by
the War Memorial and leads over the grass to
Towan Head.*

*If you do not have sufficient time to visit
the Head, you can continue the route by
turning south from the old lifeboat house,
along the fence of the large Headlands Hotel.
The Path runs above Fistral Beach along the
golf course boundary.*

*You then follow the road and path going
round Pentire Point East. For the Crantock
Ferry turn right down steep steps in Riverside
Crescent near Fern Pit Café (Spring Bank
Holiday to mid-Sept., daily 10am-6pm). At
low tide, there are two foot-bridges up-stream.
If walking outside the ferry periods or the
bridges are covered, take the alternative path
that leads to the A3075 and Trevemper
Bridge. Continue by lane and footpath to
Penpol and Crantock Beach. Follow the Coast
Path above Crantock Beach and across the
sand dunes. There is then a track, leading
between houses and the cliff edge, to fields
and Pentire Point West. The Path descends
to an unspoiled cove, Porth Joke. A steep
climb on the other side brings you to Kelsey
Head and its Iron Age cliff castle with a
single rampart.*

En route along Holywell Bay, you pass
the Holywell — a cave with a spring, the
water from which was thought to have
curative properties. The Bay has a fine
surfing beach.

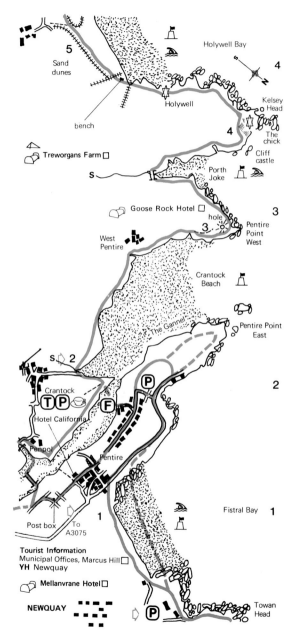

Section 18

HOLYWELL–PERRANPORTH

4½ miles (7¼km); moderate

Cum. 75¾ miles (122km)

For almost 2 miles (3¼km), the Coast Path encircles the perimeter of the Penhale military area. The main attraction of the village itself is the 600-year old pub, The Treguth.

The Path is signposted from the car park by the south side of the bridge over the stream in Holywell and continues along the outside of the military perimeter fence for 200 yards before crossing the fence by a stile and steps. Notices warn you to keep to the track marked by white posts and not to attempt short cuts. The Path climbs to the 200-foot (60m) cliff-top with a good view of Carter's or Gull Rocks and Perran Bay. There is another sign warning that firing takes place when the red flag is flying; the sentry will indicate the path when this is happening. The going is over turf with many wild flowers in spring.

The Path turns inland to skirt Hoblyn's Cove and here the Path is fenced in for about 300 yards (275m) as it runs close to the hutted camp. You pass a number of old mine shafts. After rounding Ligger Point, the Path drops down gradually to the sands of Perran Bay and along the foot of the sandhills to Perranporth.

Just before the holiday camp in the sandhills is a track leading inland to St Piran's Oratory ½ mile (¾km) away. The remains of the 8th-century chapel have now been buried in the sand to protect it against vandalism. It is said to be the site of the cell of St. Piran, Irish missionary and patron saint of Cornwall. A short distance to the north-east, across the dunes, is the site of the 12th-century St Piran's church and a granite cross mentioned in a 10th century document. The Cross near the church is modern. Perranporth (Port of Piran) is an attractive small resort.

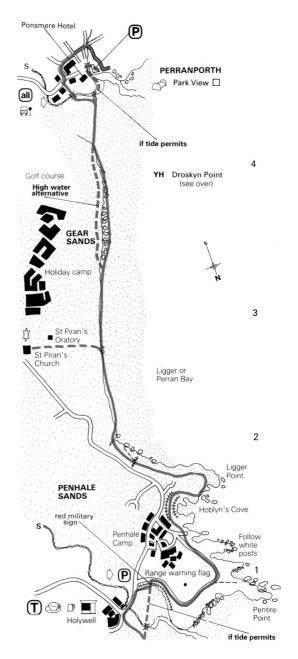

36

Section 19
PERRANPORTH–ST AGNES
4 miles (6½km); moderate
Cum. 79¾ miles (128¼km)

Take the road which climbs along the south side of Perran Beach, the start of some fine cliff-walking through what used to be a flourishing copper and tin mining area. A path takes you on to a road past the large Droskyn Castle holiday centre and the youth hostel. At the side of the fence, a narrow path leads up to the heath-covered cliff-top, round Droskyn Point and along the cliff, 250 feet (75m) above the sea, with a sheer drop below.

On Cligga Head the Path passes through a disused quarry area with large boulders showing the strata of the granite. There are good views from various points along the coast here. From this area southwards, on the Path, there is much evidence of the former flourishing copper and tin mining activity in the form of abandoned mine shafts and engine houses. Most mines had only a few years of life during the second half of the 19th century.

After the walk up from Trevellas Porth, with its ruined mine, there is a drop almost at once to Trevaunance Cove, the nearest beach to St Agnes, ¾ mile (1km) up the road inland.

Trevaunance Cove, formerly a small harbour, had all its installations swept away by storms. The beach is sandy and the sea is suitable for surfing. There is a pub on the water-front.

St Agnes, with its precipitous streets, derelict mines and rows of houses — homes of miners 100 years ago — is now a place for retired folk and holidaymakers. It has considerable charm, part of which is Stippy Stappy Lane, the name probably meaning very steep. There are four good pubs.

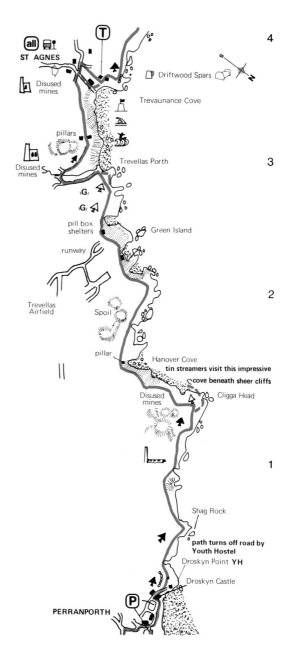

Section 20
NEWDOWNS HEAD-
PORTHTOWAN

3½ miles (5½km); moderate
Cum. 83¼ miles (134km)

Rounding St Agnes Head you have the start of some excellent cliff-walking noted for its fine views and wildlife. There are the occasional gaunt remains of an engine house or mine workings.

As far as the wildlife is concerned, St Agnes Head itself has the largest breeding colony of kittiwakes in the area, estimated at 900 pairs. Other breeding sea-birds on the cliffs include herring-gull, fulmar and guillemot. Grey seals can be seen at most times, basking or 'bottling' (standing up in the water, watching the watcher!). In the summer you may see the harmless basking-shark. Migrating birds that may be seen over the water include skuas, petrels, shearwaters and diving gannets. Among the flowers that add colour to the scene in their season are thrift, sea campion, birdsfoot trefoil and spring squill. Grayling and common blue butterflies feed on the vegetation where lizards and even adders lurk, making off quickly when they detect footsteps.

Passing the engine-house of the Towanroath Mine perched below the cliff-top, you then come to Chapel Porth with a sandy cove between high rocks. A fine expanse of sand is left by the retreating tide. The disused Wheal Charlotte Mine lies near the Path about ½ mile (¾km) before Porthtowan.

Porthtowan is a developing resort with a sandy beach, surfing and two pubs.

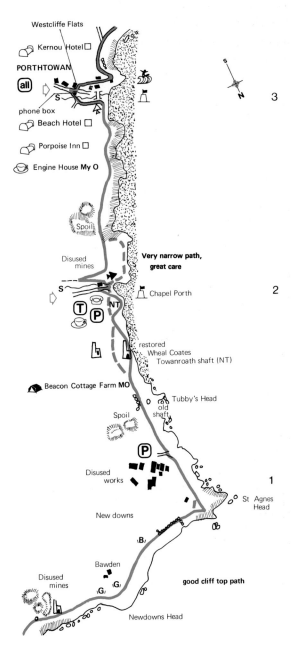

Section 21
TOBBAN HORSE-PORTREATH-CARVANNEL DOWNS
4 miles (6½km); moderate
Cum. 87¼ miles (140½km)

This is a pleasant enough stretch of the Path, with two stiff climbs but having to walk for nearly 2 miles (3¼km) a few inches from the fence of the Nancekuke Defence Area detracts somewhat from the enjoyment.

From Porthtowan the route of the Path will be seen climbing easily to the cliff-top, initially along a by-road and then a track, passing some mine shafts. Shortly afterwards you have to drop down steeply to the bottom of a cleft, where the stream makes a small waterfall. Then scramble up the other side. The Path hugs the fence of the Nancekuke Defence Area, sometimes wedged narrowly between the fence and the cliff edge. Eventually the fence boundary is reached. The Path continues to the entrance road of the Defence Establishment. You can either follow this road down into Portreath or the path by the car park, round the cliff, past the Daymark tower into the town.

Portreath is another former busy harbour, serving the mining area of nearby Redruth. It is now a resort with good sands and a surfing beach. There are two pubs: The Portreath and The Basset. The new housing area near the harbour is surprisingly attractive.

To rejoin the Coast Path, take the narrow country-road leading off the main road to the south of the harbour. This leads past some pleasant houses to a footpath climbing through a green valley and round Tregea Hill to the cliff. From here for 6 miles (9¾km) west is National Trust land.

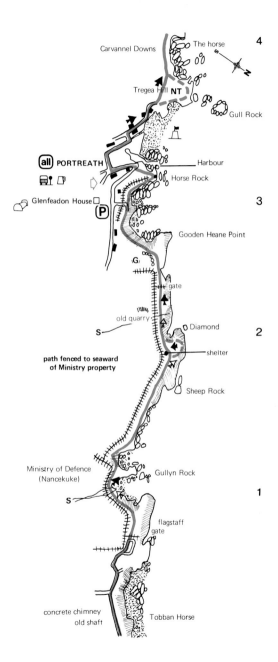

Section 22

CARVANNEL DOWNS-
HELL'S MOUTH

4 miles (6½km); easy

Cum. 91¼ miles (146¾km)

The Path takes a steep drop into a cove with a small stream and a waterfall. This part of the cliffs is known as Carvannel Downs.

Below the cliff, at the head of a narrow inlet, before reaching Carvannel Downs, a cave known as Ralph's Cupboard was used as a smugglers' storehouse. Samphire Island, just off the coast, was formerly the source of the samphire herb, gathered for food and pickling.

Carvannel Downs give way to Reskajeage Downs and the Coast Path continues over gorse and turf along this splendid stretch of high cliff. To the west of Samphire Island is Basset's Cove, accessible by a steep path. About 1 mile (1½km) farther on, the main road runs close to the cliff edge but a track has been made to take the Coast Path away from the road. The route then turns and follows the coast over the gorse until reaching the awe-inspiring cleft, Hell's Mouth. You will usually find a number of sightseers here in the season as the B3301 road is so near. From Hell's Mouth, the Path turns north-west towards Navax Point.

Navax Point is another good spot for observing birds in passage. Usually flying west in summer and autumn, there are shearwaters, gannets and fulmars, sometimes in large numbers. The caves below the Point are breeding places for the grey seal. The cliffs themselves are notable for flowers and plants: in the spring bluebells and spring squills abound.

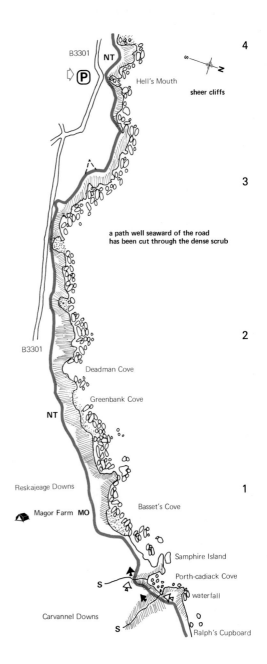

B3301

NT

Hell's Mouth

sheer cliffs

4

3

a path well seaward of the road
has been cut through the dense scrub

B3301

2

Deadman Cove

Greenbank Cove

NT

1

Reskajeage Downs

Basset's Cove

Magor Farm MO

Samphire Island

Porth-cadiack Cove

waterfall

S

Carvannel Downs

S

Ralph's Cupboard

Section 23
NAVAX POINT–THE TOWANS
4¾ miles (7¾km); easy
Cum. 96 miles (154½km)

From Navax Point the Path takes you round Godrevy Point.

As you follow the Path round the Point, with the unmanned automatic lighthouse on Godrevy Island, the scene may look peaceful enough but the Stones, a dangerous reef just below the surface, caused many frightful wrecks before (and some after) the lighthouse was built in 1859. The combination of northerly gales and the Stones usually proved fatal. In 1649, a ship crammed with the possessions of the refugee Prince of Wales, later Charles II, sank on the rocks the day that his father was executed, losing all but three of the crew. People on shore enriched themselves with the loot. Also tragic was the wrecking of the packet steamer, *The Nile*, on the reef in 1854 with the loss of all passengers and crew.

Having rounded the Point, there is a refreshment hut (open in the season) at the National Trust boundary. The Path turns inland, crossing the Red River, so named from the red-stained waste from the mines of Redruth.

The novelist, Josephine Tey, donated land at Godrevy and it was the scene of one of Virginia Woolf's novels, *To the Lighthouse*.

Walk for ½ mile (¾km) to the charming village, Gwithian, with its thatched cottages and old church. In the churchyard lie many victims of shipwrecks in the Bay. The local pub is The Pendarves Arms.

At the Gwithian entrance sign, there is a coast path sign leading off to the right into the dunes. Follow the posts all the way through the dunes for the next 3 miles to Black Cliff. The beach is popular for surfing and water ski-ing. The Towans (dunes) are dotted with chalets and bungalows but the sands are pleasant.

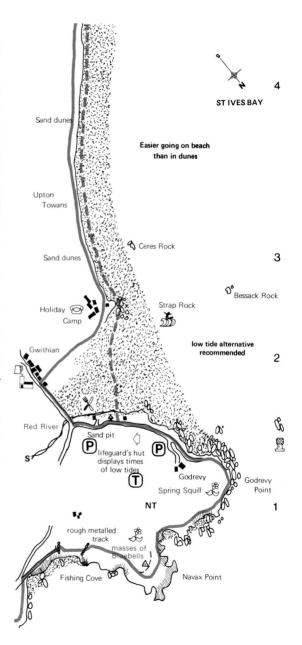

ST IVES BAY

Sand dunes

Easier going on beach than in dunes

Upton Towans

Ceres Rock

Sand dunes

Bessack Rock

Holiday Camp

Strap Rock

Gwithian

low tide alternative recommended

Red River

Sand pit

lifeguard's hut displays times of low tides

Godrevy

Spring Squill

Godrevy Point

NT

rough metalled track

masses of Bluebells

Fishing Cove

Navax Point

4

3

2

1

41

Section 24

HAYLE–
PORTHKIDNEY SANDS

5¾ miles (9¼km); easy

Cum. 101¾ miles (163¾km)

Apart from the last mile, the Path has to take to the road round the Hayle estuary, not an attractive route. The estuary is, however, a good area for bird life. The Path skirts the bungalows at the west end of the sands, crossing the canal bridge and on to the busy road in Hayle. You continue on this road to Lelant.

The Carnsew Pool provides a diversion for those keen to watch the birds (see p.16). There is a bus service from Hayle to St Ives, also a rail service (from St Erth railway station).

Continuing along the road, turn off up the A3074 towards Lelant. A short way up the hill the Path takes a turning on the right by a roadside cross down a pleasant by-road eventually bringing you along the railway and the shore of the estuary. Pass Lelant rail Halt to come to Green Lane and Lelant church.

The church of St Uny is mainly 15th-century but has earlier parts including a fine Norman arch. There are two ancient Cornish crosses in the churchyard. St Ives used to come under St Uny parish.

Leaving the churchyard, the Path crosses the golf course and goes under a rail bridge before turning along the railway above Porthkidney Sands, dangerous for bathing but a good place for sea birds, including terns, in the autumn.

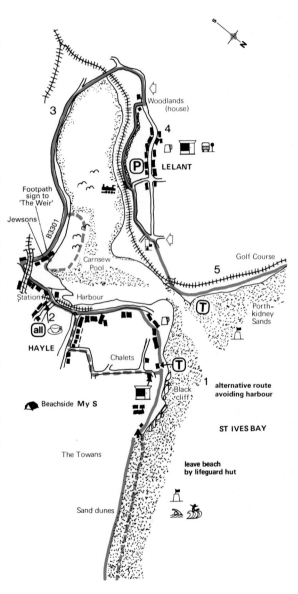

42

Section 25

PORTHKIDNEY SANDS-
ST IVES

2¼ miles (3½km); easy

Cum. 104 miles (167¼km)

*From above Porthkidney Beach, the Coast
Path proceeds by a good cliff route alongside
the railway until, at Carbis Bay station, it
takes to the roadway leading past the Carbis
Bay Hotel. Once past the hotel, the Path goes
over the railway and follows it closely.
Crossing over the line again it drops down to
Porthminster Beach and the harbour.*

St Ives (pop. 9,900) is one of the best
known Cornish resorts. Fishermen's
cottages are packed closely up the slope
from the harbour and, above, are those
of the miners who worked in the nearby
mines in the 1800s. Along the approaches
from the south, are the prosperous villas
and hotels of the residential quarter,
enjoying fine views of the sea. The town
is named after the Irish St Ia who landed
here in AD460 on a Christian mission. In
1487 Henry VII granted the right for the
town to hold a market and two fairs. Its
livelihood depended on pilchard fishing
until the 1890s when the coming of the
railway made it a popular holiday and
residential town. The parish church of St
Ia is 15th-century. Smeaton, famous
builder of the Eddystone Lighthouse,
constructed the harbour in 1770. The
station is the terminus of the branch line
from the main London-Penzance line.
There is a museum, Information Office
and four excellent beaches: Carbis Bay,
Porthminster, Porthgwidden and
Porthmeor which is suitable for surfing.
St Ives is a fine spot for bird-watching,
especially during migrations. To avoid
parking difficulties in St Ives you can
park at Lelant railway station and go by
train to St Ives — a pleasant journey of 4
miles (6½km). The parking charge
includes rail fare. Available May - Sept.

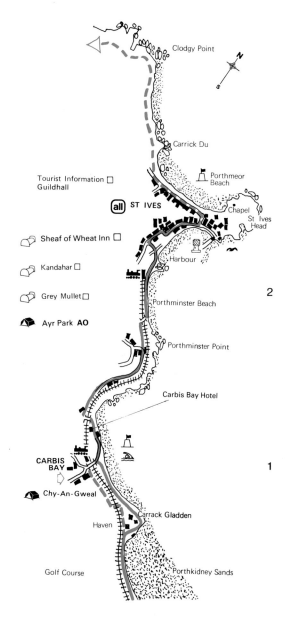

Clodgy Point

Carrick Du

Tourist Information □
Guildhall

Porthmeor
Beach

all ST IVES

Chapel

St Ives
Head

Sheaf of Wheat Inn □

Harbour

Kandahar □

2

Grey Mullet□

Porthminster Beach

Ayr Park **AO**

Porthminster Point

Carbis Bay Hotel

1

CARBIS
BAY

Chy-An-Gweal

Carrack Gladden

Haven

Golf Course

Porthkidney Sands

Section 26

ST IVES-MUSSEL POINT

3½ miles (5½km); strenuous

Cum. 107½ miles (173km)

The best known St Ives figure of recent times was Barbara Hepworth, the famous sculptor who found enduring inspiration in the Cornish landscape. Yorkshire-born, she moved from London in 1939 to St Ives and remained there for the rest of her life. She was an outstanding artist of the same school of abstract sculpture as her friend, Henry Moore. One of Barbara Hepworth's most moving works is the memorial in the parish church, to her son, Paul, killed in Malaya in 1953 while serving in the RAF. She died tragically in a fire in 1975 in her studio, Trewyn. Trewyn has been left to the nation and contains fine examples of her work. Visiting hours are: **Jul. and Aug.** Mon.-Sat., 10am to 6.30pm, Sun. 2pm to 6pm. **Apr., Jun. and Sept.** Mon.-Sat. 10am to 6.30pm, closed Sun.. **Oct.-Mar.** weekdays 10am to 4pm, closed Sun.. Trewyn is in Barnnoon Hill, near the High Street.

To join the Coast Path in St Ives follow Fore Street and the sign to Porthmeor Beach up from the centre of the town. This skirts the putting-green above the beach, leading on to the cliff Path. There are no refreshment facilities until Zennor (Section 27).

The Path westwards from St Ives crosses bare, open country. It follows closely the line of the cliffs, over furze-covered, boulder-strewn moorland. The going is fairly level but where the route dips down to the coves it becomes steep. There are magnificent views from the Trig Point 300 feet (90m) above Carn Naun. Shortly after, a steep descent takes you close to the water's edge, with a chance to watch sea-birds, and often seals, on The Carracks, two islets just off the shore. The Path then crosses the gorse and bracken, passing Mussel Point.

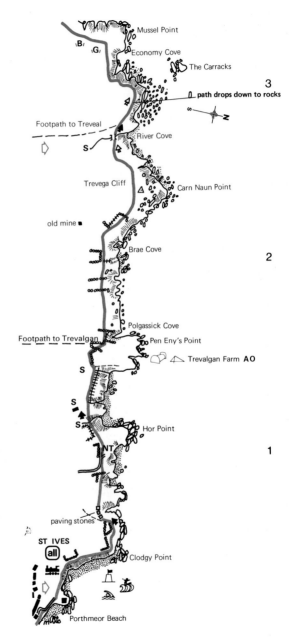

Mussel Point
Economy Cove
The Carracks
3
path drops down to rocks
Footpath to Treveal
River Cove
Trevega Cliff
Carn Naun Point
old mine
Brae Cove
2
Polgassick Cove
Footpath to Trevalgan
Pen Eny's Point
Trevalgan Farm **A O**
Hor Point
1
NT
paving stones
ST IVES
all
Clodgy Point
Porthmeor Beach

Section 27
MUSSEL POINT–
PORTHMEOR COVE
4¼ miles (6¾km); strenuous
Cum. 111¾ miles (179¾km)

Rounding the Wicca Pool, the Path continues along the cliff, turns inland to negotiate the steep combe formed by the stream from Tremedda Farm to the sea and then brings you to Zennor Head which is 300 feet (90m) high. The cliffs drop sheer, cut by numerous deep clefts.

From Zennor Head, a public path leads inland for ½ mile (¾km) to Zennor (St Sinare), a small village and convenient refreshment stop. The little church is 15th-century with some parts dating from the 13th century and contains a bench-end with a carving of the Mermaid of Zennor, said to have lured the squire's son into the sea at Pendour Cove where his voice can still be heard singing to his love. In the churchyard are two 9th-century Cornish stone crosses. The Wayside Museum, below The Tinners' Arms, housed in an old mill, contains a collection illustrating Cornish life from prehistoric days. The museum is open 10am to 6pm from Whitsun to the end of September; Refreshments are available.

For those interested in archaeology, there is a ¾ mile (1km) detour inland to Zennor Quoit, a 4,500-year-old Neolithic chamber tomb with a main chamber of five large upright stones and an antechamber of three others.

The Path from Zennor Head skirts Pendour and Porthglaze Coves, approaching Gurnard's Head.

On the Head are remains of an Iron Age cliff castle with traces of three ramparts and hut circles. The Porthmeor Courtyard Village (1st–5th centuries AD) is 1 mile (1½km) south-east from Porthmeor Point. Permission to visit is required from Porthmeor Farm.

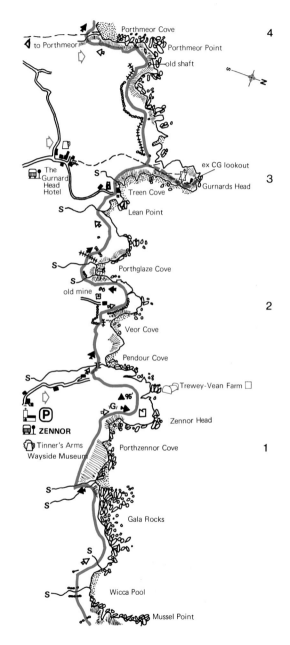

Section 28

PORTHMEOR COVE–
PENDEEN WATCH

4 miles (6½km); strenuous
Cum. 115¾ miles (186¼km)

The Path, on leaving Porthmeor Cove, climbs the headland on the tip of which is another cliff castle, the Iron Age Bosigran Castle, with a stone rampart across its neck.

The derelict engine-houses along this route are signs of one of the mining areas for which Cornwall is noted. The coast westward — apart from Porthmeor to Portheras, where it is granite to the cliff edge — is strewn with traces of mining.

Inland from Morvah Cliff is the hamlet of Morvah, reached by following a sunken path for ½ mile (¾km). The 15th-century Morvah church was restored in 1828. There is a bus service to St Just and Penzance.

Pendeen Watch Lighthouse (Pendeen meaning 'fortified headland') was completed in 1900 and can be visited in the afternoons. Gales from both the south-west and north-west, fog, the rocky coast and its fringe of reefs, produced a high incidence of wrecks, some without survivors, during the increase in traffic, following the introduction of steam and increasing coal exports from South Wales. The terrible gale in January 1939 was particularly tragic. The St Ives lifeboat with seven of its eight-man crew was lost and the gale also claimed the lives of all hands on the collier *Wilston* which sank off Wicca Pool.

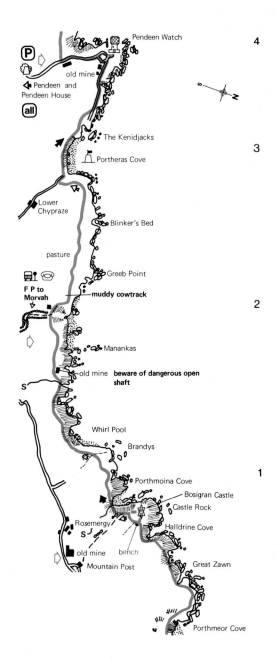

Section 29
PENDEEN WATCH-
CAPE CORNWALL
4 miles (6½km); moderate
Cum. 119¾ miles (192¾km)

From Pendeen Watch Lighthouse, follow the road inland for ¼ mile (400m) past a row of cottages; the Coast Path is signposted at the edge of the road. Dropping down a small valley and, crossing the stream by a footbridge, you climb the cliff ahead passing through the former Levant Mine.

Pendeen House, ¼ mile (400m) down the road past the Coast Path turn-off, was the home of Dr William Borlase (1695-1772), father of Cornish archaeology. Behind Pendeen House is an Iron Age fogou — an underground chamber. Ask at the house for permission to visit.

The Levant Mine produced copper and tin ore until its closure in 1919 after 31 miners were killed in an accident. The Mine ran for 1 mile (1½km) under the sea. One of its steam beam-engines, built in 1840, can be visited on application to the Geevor Mine (tel:01736-788662) which has recently ceased production.

The Path continues past the much-photographed Crowns Mine and then the Botallack, closed in 1914 after over 100 years' activity. Both mined copper and tin ore. The village of Botallack, ½ mile (¾km) inland, is a good place for refreshment or accommodation.

The Coast Path turns inland at Kenidjack Cliff to cross the valley of the stream which flows into Porth Ledden Cove and takes you to Cape Cornwall.

On the cliff is Kenidjack Cliff Castle with ramparts and ditch.

Cape Cornwall is only a short distance east of Land's End. The chimney on the summit was part of the Cape Cornwall Mine (closed 1870).

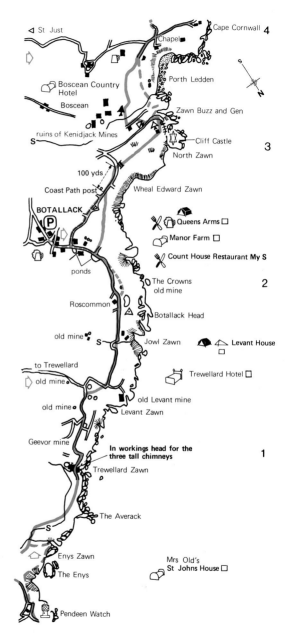

Section 30
CAPE CORNWALL-
WHITESAND BAY
4 miles (6½km); moderate
Cum. 123¾ miles (199¼km)

From Cape Cornwall, the Path follows an unmetalled road to the top of Carn Gloose.

Follow the unmetalled road, where it turns inland, for 100 yards (90m) and you come, on the right, to the chambered cairn of Carn Gloose or Ballowal (rhymes with fowl), one of Cornwall's most mysterious sites. A domed chamber 15 feet (4½m) high with walls 4 feet (1¼m) thick was built over a 7-foot (2m) deep pit cut in the rock. Completely sealed from the outside, it is thought to be a religious shrine. There was a stone wall round the structure and an entrance grave on the south side. It could be Neolithic. Pottery found here is of the Bronze Age.

St Just, a mile inland on the same road, was named after a Breton missionary monk. Near the central square is an open-air theatre (Plen an Gwary meaning 'playing place') used until the 17th century for miracle plays in Cornish. Four similar sites survive in the county. St Just church has two mediaeval wall paintings and a 5th-or 6th-century stone inscribed in Latin on one side: *Selus Ic Jacet* (Selus lies here) and, on the other side, there is a cross which indicates it is a very early Christian monument.

From Carn Gloose, walk down through the bracken to the road below (turn left for the Land's End Youth Hostel). Follow the road down to Porth Nanven beach, from which the Path continues midway between cliff-top and sea. You soon come to Whitesand Bay, a sandy beach over 1 mile (1½km) long, popular for bathing and surfing, but watch for warning signs.

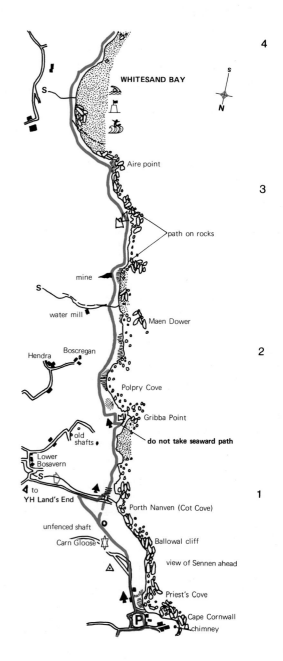

WHITESAND BAY

Aire point

path on rocks

mine

water mill

Maen Dower

Hendra   Boscregan

Polpry Cove

Gribba Point

old shafts

do not take seaward path

Lower Bosavern

to YH Land's End

Porth Nanven (Cot Cove)

unfenced shaft

Carn Gloose

Ballowal cliff

view of Sennen ahead

Priest's Cove

Cape Cornwall

chimney

Section 31

WHITESAND BAY-
LAND'S END-BLACK CARN

4 miles (6½km); moderate

Cum. 127¾ miles (205½km)

The Path follows round Whitesand Bay into Sennen Cove, a former fishing village and now a small resort. Buses go to Land's End and Penzance. The route continues where the road round the harbour finishes at an old circular capstan house, then goes up past the Coast Guard look-out.

You are now in granite country and you can see the sheer rock pillars contrasting with the more rounded slatey cliffs sloping down to the sea, still in view behind you. Between the Path and the cliff-edge, 500 yards (460m) south of the look-out, is Maen (meaning 'stone') Castle, an early cliff castle dating back to 300BC.

Dr Syntax Head, the most westerly point of the UK, is the true 'land's end' but, passing the 'First and Last House' you come to Land's End itself.

In season, Land's End has everything: hotel, shops, souvenirs, snack-bar, post-box and car park. Land's End (Pedn an Laaz meaning 'end of earth'), a world-famous landmark, is mentioned as Belerion by the 2nd-century Ptolemy.

The Longships Lighthouse can be seen 1½ miles (2½km) away. In clear weather, the Wolf Rock Lighthouse may be seen and even the Scilly Isles, 28 miles (45km) to the south-west.

From Land's End you have some of the finest scenery of the Coast Path — a good cliff-top track, well defined in most parts, over boulder-strewn grass and heather but it affords little shelter in rough weather.

The rocky isle, Armed Knight, shows again the castellated granite.

Beyond Mill Bay, the Path continues past Carn Lês Boel, round Pendower Cove to Black Carn.

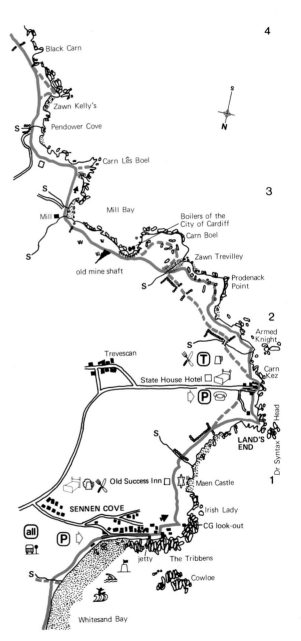

49

Section 32

BLACK CARN-PENBERTH

4 miles (6½km); moderate

Cum. 131¾ miles (212km)

The Path here provides magnificent cliff-walking. Continuing past the Coast Guard look-out, you round Gwennap Head with its 'funnel' near the cliff edge caused by the collapse of a cave. Take care. From Porthgwarra, the Path skirts Porthchapel with its small sandy beach. Water from the Holy Well of St Levan is still used for baptisms. Ancient stone steps lead down from here to the beach.

St Levan, ¼ mile (400m) inland, is named after the 5th-century Breton saint, St Selevan. The church is Norman with a fine Celtic cross in the churchyard.

Just beyond Pedn-Men-An-Mere ('great rock headland') is the Minack Open Air Theatre. It was founded in the 1930s by Rowena Cade in her front garden, with the auditorium built into the cliff, facing the sea. A performance in this magnificent setting is an unforgettable experience but take a cushion and a rug!

Porthcurno (Port of Cornwall) was the terminus of the Eastern Cable Co., including the first India-UK link in 1870.

Steep steps lead from the theatre down to the beach of minute white shells and Rowena Cade's tiny beach house. The Path climbs to the cliff-top opposite. The white pyramid by the Path is a guide for shipping and marks where the first transatlantic cable came ashore in 1880. The well-defined Path leads to the headland Treryn Dinas (fortress settlement) with an Iron Age cliff castle. Also on the headland is the Logan Rock, an 80-ton (81¼ tonne) rocking stone!

Treen, ½ mile (¾km) inland, is an attractive village, with The Logan Rock pub and a post office store.

. *The Path continues to Penberth Cove, where the National Trust ensures that the cottages are let to local workers.*

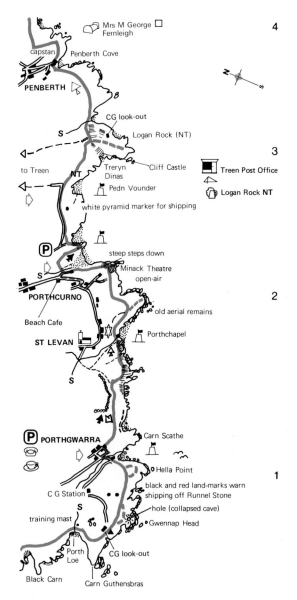

Section 33
PENBERTH-LAMORNA
3½ miles (5½km); stren. /moderate
Cum. 135¼ miles (217¾km)

Notice the vegetation changes on this more sheltered coast. Where the Path drops through a small wood to the water's edge at St Loy, it is almost tropical. The Path here runs for about 50 yards (45m) along the beach and then climbs behind a large boulder. The going is reasonable once past Boscawen Point. A short section of unmetalled road leads to Tater Du.

The automatic lighthouse at Tater Du was built in 1965 after a series of tragic shipwrecks. Just beyond, the Path crosses the property of the writer, Derek Tangye.

From Carn Barges the Path runs close to the cliff edge to Lamorna, an attractive village which is quite an artists' colony, with Post Office stores and The Lamorna Inn, known locally as 'The Wink'.

The nickname goes back to the time when, for £20 anyone could open an alehouse such as this. Spirits were barred but a wink would produce smuggled brandy, as shown on the sign!

A few yards up the road from the inn, a path on the left leads for ½ mile (¾km) to the B3315 and three important archaeological sites. Turn left for ¼ mile (400m) and, in a field on the left, is the Merry Maidens Stone Circle (possibly from Meur Maen meaning Great Stone), a complete circle of 19 stones, dating from the Bronze Age. A short way on, by the roadside, is the Tregiffian Entrance Grave with remains of a Bronze Age cremation, discovered during road-widening operations. Going back along the road for ½ mile (¾km), in a field on the left are the Pipers, two Bronze Age standing stones, 12 feet (3½m) high, said to represent the two who played for the Merry Maidens to dance on a Sunday and were turned to stone.

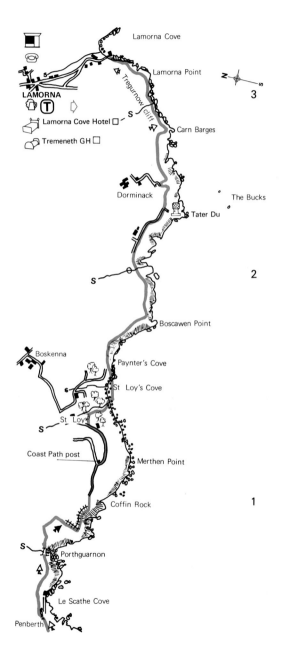

51

Section 34
CARN DU-MOUSEHOLE-
NEWLYN
3¼ miles (5¼km); easy
Cum. 138½ miles (222¾km)

A climb out of Lamorna brings you to the headland, Carn Du. The Path then turns slightly inland through a small wood. It climbs steeply to the Coast Guard look-out and then along a metalled path affording a fine view into Mousehole. From here the route is along the main road to Newlyn. If you wish to avoid this, turn off at Raginnis Farm and by-pass Mousehole. Alternatively, turn up opposite The Lobster Pot pub in Mousehole; then on to the footpath on the right at Treen Villas.

Mousehole (pronounced Mowzel) during the Middle Ages was an important fishing port but now largely depends on the visitor for its income. The houses and buildings retain their former character. The curious name is thought to be derived from a cave-mouth in the cliff to the south of the town. Mousehole was almost destroyed by Spanish raiders in 1595.

The village of Paul was burned down in 1595. In the church of St Paul is a monument to Dolly Pentreath who died in 1778. She is said to be the last person to speak Cornish as her mother tongue.

From Paul, a good footpath leads you beside Penlee Quarry — an important source of stone for roads and railway ballast — to Newlyn.

Due to its excellent harbour, Newlyn has survived as Cornwall's largest fishing town. Parts of the harbour date from the 15th century.

Newlyn also suffered at the hands of the Spaniards in 1595. It is famous as an artists' colony, many well-known artists having had their studios there.

There is a frequent bus service between Newlyn and Penzance along the main road.

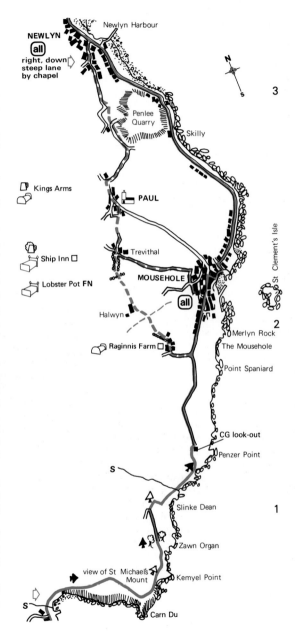

52

Section 35

PENZANCE–
ST MICHAEL'S MOUNT

4 miles (6½km); easy

Cum. 142½ miles (229¼km)

Leaving Penzance by the main A30, there is a footbridge over the railway ½ mile (¾km) down the road, opposite the Heliport. The Path runs on the beach round Mount's Bay above high-water mark. There is a bus to Marazion, if preferred. Marazion Marsh on the approaches to the town is noted for its wintering wild fowl.

Marazion earned the privilege of holding a fair in the early Middle Ages before Penzance did so.

Most people will wish to visit St Michael's Mount, linked with Marazion at low tide by a causeway. There is a ferry service to the Mount in the summer. Originally a Benedictine monastery, the Mount was founded by Edward the Confessor in honour of the saint and as a dependence of the great Abbey of Mont St Michel in Brittany. Suppressed in 1425, it became a fortress and a residence. Since 1659, the Mount has been the seat of the St Aubyn family whose descendent, Lord St Aubyn, still lives there. He gave the Mount to the National Trust in 1954. It is generally identified with the Ictis mentioned by Diodorus Siculus (1st century BC) as the port from which tin was shipped to Brittany.

The Castle is open to visitors: **Apr.–May.** Mon.–Fri. except Thurs.; **Jun.–Oct.** Mon.–Fri.; **Nov.–Mar.** guided tours only on certain days. The café is open in the summer. For information tel: (01736) 710507.

To rejoin the Path, follow the main road for 1 mile (1½km). A Coast Path signpost points down a track to the right. Alternatively you can take a bus out of town: ask for Henfor Terrace.

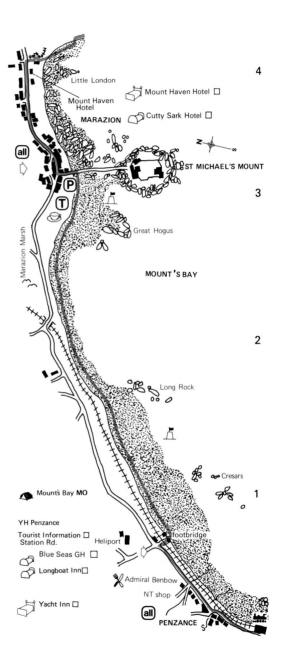

Little London

Mount Haven Hotel □

Mount Haven Hotel

Cutty Sark Hotel □

MARAZION

ST MICHAEL'S MOUNT

Marazion Marsh

Great Hogus

MOUNT'S BAY

Long Rock

Cresars

Mount's Bay MO

YH Penzance

Tourist Information □
Station Rd.

Heliport

footbridge

Blue Seas GH □

Longboat Inn□

Admiral Benbow

NT shop

Yacht Inn □

PENZANCE

Section 36
TRENOW COVE–PRAA SANDS
4 miles (6½km); moderate
Cum. 146½ miles (235¾km)

The Path drops down to the rocky beach for 100 yds and then up metal steps. It then continues alongside fields to Maen-du (Black Rock) Point and Perran Sands.

A path leads inland for ¼ mile (400m) to Perranuthnoe, usually known as 'Perran'. There is a 15th-century church and The Victoria Inn is recommended.

Alternatively you can walk along Perran Sands. The route then follows the cliff edge, emerging on the wide sweep above Stackhouse Cove with a view of Cudden Point. After rounding Cudden Point you reach Prussia Cove, a delightful spot, particularly out of season.

The name Prussia Cove comes from the King of Prussia Inn which formerly stood on the cliff. This was a popular name when Frederick the Great was an ally during the Seven Years' War. The inn was kept by the Carters, famous 18th-century smugglers. It is said they mounted a small battery of guns to defy Customs. The most colourful member, Captain Harry Carter, fled to New York where he became a Methodist. He returned to Roscoff, was imprisoned during the Revolution and released to a more settled life in 1795.

Prussia Cove saw the largest wreck in Cornwall when, in 1947, the battleship *Warspite*, on the way to the breakers' yard, was blown on to the rocks. A concrete pillar on the Point is a remnant of the salvage operation. Bessy's Cove — after Bessy Burrow who kept an alehouse nearby — was the landing place for smuggled brandy.

The route of the Path then continues across the bracken-covered cliff top above Kenneggy Sands. Pass Hoe Point, with one or two climbs, to reach Praa Sands, a long stretch of safe, sandy beach with bungalows and caravans.

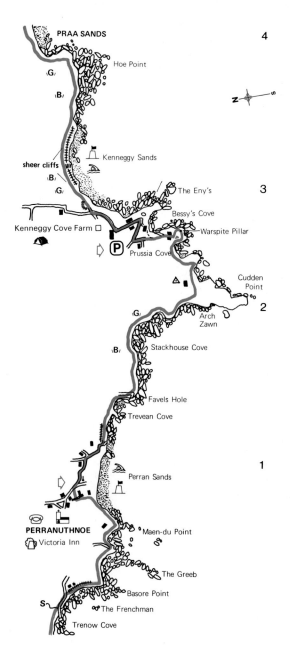

Section 37

PRAA SANDS–TREGAR POINT

3¼ miles (5¼km); moderate

Cum. 149¾ miles (241km)

At Praa Sands you have all the facilities for food, refreshment, accommodation and parking. The official route is along the beach for 100 yds, up the steps and immediately above the beach, then through the sandhills. There is an exit at the east end of the sands to Lesceave Cliff (National Trust). The Path continues through the bracken to Rinsey Head, a climb that starts a spectacular stretch of cliff-walking, skirting deep clefts.

Follow the Path from the Head on an unmetalled road for a short way to the shell of the engine-house and chimney of the Wheal Prosper Mine. The short life of this copper mine ended in 1860. The structure has been strengthened to ensure preservation.

A path leads from the mine to Rinsey Cove, which geologists find of special interest. From just south of Penzance to Praa Sands, the coastal rocks are slates but, here, for a few miles they are granite again and, as would be expected, we find mining activity at the edge of the formation. At Tregonning Hill 2 miles (3¼km) inland, in 1746, china-clay (decomposed granite) was found for the first time in Britain, only 200 yards (180m) from granite in its unaltered state—a small beginning to the thriving industry we encounter farther along the coast. Cornwall's deposits of china-clay are the deepest in the world.

20 yds after the engine house, fork right and continue halfway down the cliff round Trewavas Head. Next, in an impressive setting, are the ruins of the engine-house of Wheal Trewavas, which mined copper ore under the sea until 1850 when the sea broke in.

To Tregear Point the line of the Path is clear and diverted from dangerous cliff edges. There is a good view here of herring gulls and fulmars in the nesting season.

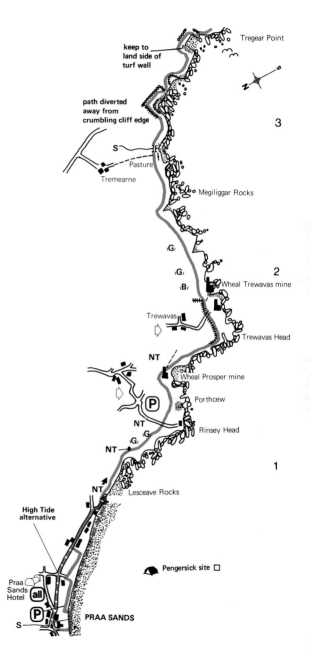

Tregear Point

keep to land side of turf wall

path diverted away from crumbling cliff edge

3

S

Pasture

Tremearne

Megiliggar Rocks

\G\

\G\

\G\

\B\

2

Wheal Trewavas mine

Trewavas

Trewavas Head

NT

Wheal Prosper mine

Porthcew

P

NT

G

Rinsey Head

\G\

NT

1

NT

Lesceave Rocks

High Tide alternative

Pengersick site ☐

Praa Sands Hotel (all)

P

PRAA SANDS

S

Section 38

PORTHLEVEN–
GUNWALLOE FISHING COVE

3¾ miles (6km); moderate

Cum. 153½ miles (247km)

Approaching Porthleven the, Path passes a memorial cross raised by a parson who began burying shipwreck victims in consecrated ground. Prior to this, these unfortunates were consigned to mass graves in unconsecrated ground.

On the shore, a 20-ton (20½ tonnes) boulder 10 feet (3m) long, the Giant's Rock, is formed of a kind of gneiss not found elsewhere in Britain. It may have been left behind from the Ice Age.

Porthleven (Port of St Leven) was a fishing port now dependent on the tourist trade. It is on the Falmouth to Penzance bus route. The Ship Inn is the local pub.

To regain the Coast Path climb out of the town at the far east end of the harbour, following Loe Bar Road and Mounts Road, past some old cottages and the Coast Guard look-out. This takes you through to Loe Bar. You can also walk along the sands.

Loe Bar was formed by the damming of the River Cober. The bank of shingle has since been built up by the sea. Loe Pool is a fine expanse of fresh water, part of the Penrose estate (National Trust). Walkers can enter the estate during daylight hours by the gate on the Path.

You cross Loe Bar at its narrowest area, over 600 yards (550m) of shingle, the Path continuing up an easy slope to the cliff top.

There is a memorial to Henry Trengrouse who, after witnessing the loss off Loe Bar of *HMS Anson* in 1807, invented the rocket life-saving apparatus.

Keep to the seaward fork where the track diverts inland; this leads you to Gunwalloe Fishing Cove. If the tide allows, you can walk along the beach all the way from the Bar to the Cove.

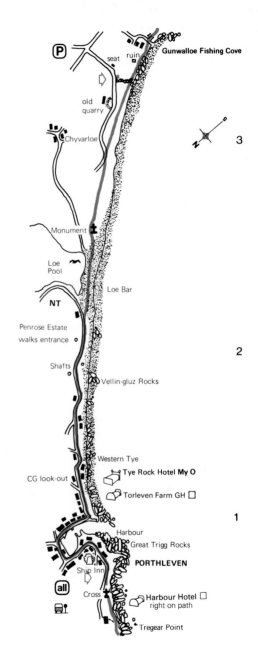

56

Section 39
GUNWALLOE COVE-
MULLION COVE
4 miles (6½km); moderate
Cum. 157½ miles (253½km)

From Gunwalloe Fishing Cove, the Path slopes up to the 200-foot (60m) cliff-top and then alongside the main road before rounding the fields of Halzephron Cliff (Hell's cliff).

The Halzephron Inn is said to have a smugglers' tunnel to the cliff below.

From the cliff, the Path descends to Church Cove, a crowded beach in summer. The little church of St Winwalloe, named after a 6th-century Breton abbot, has its tower half-buried in the sandhills. It is 15th-century with a Norman font. The manor of Winnianton — the farm on the east side of the road — is mentioned in the Domesday Book.

Church Cove is famous for its wrecks. In 1526 a Flemish, and in 1780, a Spanish treasure ship were wrecked here. Precious cargoes have been recovered but more possibly remains. Coins have been found in recent years.

Following the steep Path along the golf course you come to Poldhu ('black pool') Cove on the Helston-Lizard bus route. The Path on the far side of the Cove follows the metalled drive in front of the former Poldhu Hotel. The Marconi memorial is ahead on the cliff-top.

A sharp drop into Polurrian Cove, a steep climb up the other side and the Path takes you down to Mullion Cove, embodying all the fascination of the traditional small Cornish fishing harbour — better seen in the evening without the summer sightseers.

The fishing hamlet at the head of Mullion Cove is Porth Mellin ('mill harbour'). Mullion, is 1¼ miles (2km) up the road on the Helston-Lizard bus route.

Mullion Island, 300 yards (275m) off Mullion Cove, is a nesting-site for many sea-birds.

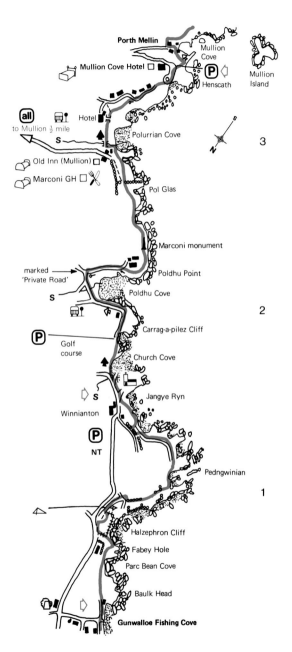

Section 40

MULLION COVE-
KYNANCE COVE

4¼ miles (7km); strenuous

Cum. 161¾ miles (260¼km)

You now approach the Lizard Peninsula, of great beauty and of interest to naturalist and geologist. The predominating rock is serpentine, used by Lizard craftsmen to create many attractive objects.

For the first mile (1½km) or so, the Path runs close to the 200-foot (60m) Mullion Cliff and rounds Predannack Head.

Here is a Nature Reserve for plants and flowers. A Victorian naturalist once claimed he found 12 species on the Lizard in the space covered by his admittedly large hat!

Down to Ogo-dour ('cave of the waters') Cove and up through bracken to join the track passing Vellan Head. Then across the moorland with only the solitary Kynance Farm in view. The white building ahead is the Lizard Lighthouse. There is a path round Vellan Head to explore if you wish.

To the cliff again at Gew Graze, where there is an outcrop of soapstone (steatite), formerly providing steatite for Wedgwood and Worcester china. A short distance further on is Pigeon Ogo (meaning cave), with views of nesting sea-birds, its crags dropping sheer to the boiling sea. The Path continues past Rill Point (the Spanish Armada was first sighted from here) and along Kynance Cliff, with a steep descent to the popular Kynance Cove, and its islands, familiar from myriad pictures. Access to the Cove can also be obtained via the A3083 toll road.

Most of the islands are a short distance off-shore and can be reached on foot over the sands within 2½ hours of low tide. Asparagus Island, Sugarloaf Rock, The Bellows and The Bishop, formed of serpentine rock, rise sheer from the sands. **Great care should be taken or you could be caught by the tide.**

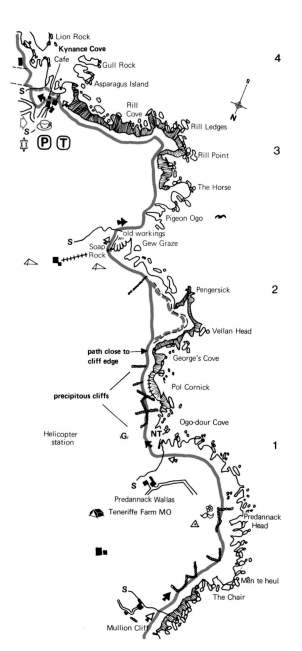

Section 41

KYNANCE COVE-LIZARD-
ENYS HEAD

5¼ miles (8½km); strenuous

Cum. 167 miles (268¾km)

From Kynance Cove, cross the footbridge over the stream and continue past the café up the steps to the top of the cliff. The Path winds ahead, past old serpentine workings to Lizard Point, the southernmost tip of Britain.

The Lizard was known to the Romans in the 2nd century. Many ships have been wrecked on the reef of rocks with hundreds of unmarked graves of victims on the cliff. The first lighthouse was built in the 17th century by Sir John Killigrew of Falmouth. The present building has a 4-million candle-power lantern. It can be visited in the afternoons.

There are paths down to Polpeor and Polbream. On the seaward side of the Path is the Lion's Den, a hole in the cliff formed one stormy night in 1847 when a cave roof collapsed. A steep path leads down to Housel Bay and its small beach. Next on the Path is a building used by Marconi in his early radio experiments. The Coast Guard station reports all shipping movements to Lloyds. The Path leads on to Kilcobben Cove and the lifeboat station. A short step and you come to Church Cove.

A short lane inland leads to Landewednack and its 15th-century church among the trees. The pillars of the 12th-century porch are of serpentine. The last sermon in Cornish was given here in 1674.

From Church Cove you pass old serpentine workings on the way to the 200-foot (60m) cliff-top. The Devil's Frying Pan, another collapsed cave roof, is 1 mile (1½km) further on. Continue down to Cadgwith with old cottages and an inn. The Path out of Cadgwith turns right, past the inn.

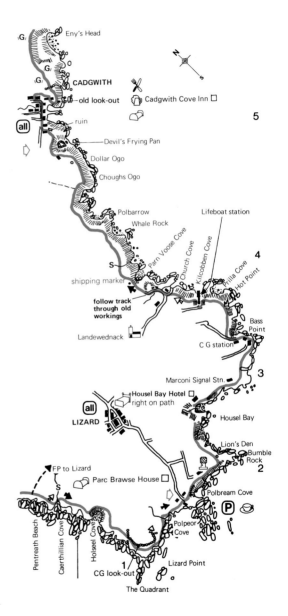

Eny's Head

CADGWITH

old look-out

Cadgwith Cove Inn

ruin

Devil's Frying Pan

Dollar Ogo

Choughs Ogo

Polbarrow

Lifeboat station

Whale Rock

Parn Voose Cove

Church Cove

Kilcobben Cove

Prilla Cove

Hot Point

shipping marker

follow track through old workings

Landewednack

Bass Point

C G station

Marconi Signal Stn.

Housel Bay Hotel

right on path

LIZARD

Housel Bay

Lion's Den

Bumble Rock

FP to Lizard

Parc Brawse House

Polbream Cove

Polpeor Cove

Pentreath Beach

Caerthillian Cove

Holseel Cove

Lizard Point

CG look-out

The Quadrant

5

4

3

2

1

Section 42
ENYS HEAD–KENNACK
SANDS–PEDN BOAR

3½ miles (5½km); mod. /strenuous
Cum. 170½ miles (274¼km)

From Enys Head the Path continues along the edge of the cliff, turning inland to negotiate the little rocky gorge at the mouth of the Poltesco valley. Continue down to Kennack Sands ½ mile (¾km) from Carleon Cove (Poltesco). Kennack Sands are popular with families and with geologists — there are exposures of four different rock types within a few yards.

Climb out of Kennack on to the eastern cliff (keep to the seaward Path from the Sands) and the going is clear. At the top of the stiff climb, you will come to Beagles Point and Pedn Boar, now owned with the farm just inland by the National Trust.

As on many stretches of the cliff Path, you may see kittiwakes here among the wheeling sea-birds. Distinguished by their cry — hence the name — and black wing tips, these are gulls which live at sea but return to the cliffs to breed.

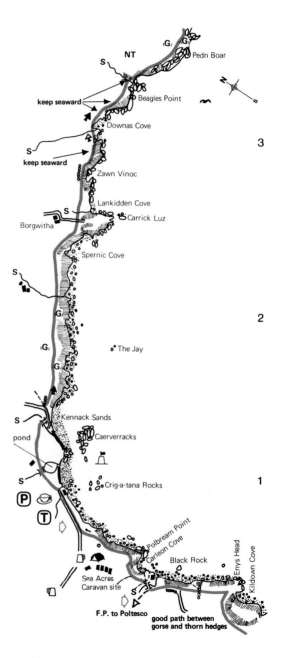

Section 43
PEDN BOAR–COVERACK–
LOWLAND POINT
4¼ miles (6¾km); moderate
Cum. 174¾ miles (281¼km)

From Pedn Boar the Path leads over Treleaver Cliff to the Coast Guard look-out on the imposing Black Head.

Near the Path on the cliff-top is the colour-testing station of British Insulated Callender's Cable Co. with panels of varying colours exposed to the weather.

From the Head, the Path turns inland across a farm track near Trewillis Farm. Then, past some outbuildings, you come to bungalows on the outskirts of Coverack. The Path carries on, bringing you out into a lane with attractive cottages. A branch of the Path runs out to Chynall's Point.

At the bottom of the steep lane is the small harbour of Coverack with its lifeboat station. The Paris Inn is named after a large liner that was stranded on this dangerous coast in 1899.

The Coast Path follows the road past the harbour and shingle beach. Where it turns inland, keep straight on, past some villas until, at the end of the road, you reach the fields. Here, there are two footpaths, the Coast Path being the seaward one. Proceed almost at sea-level as you approach Lowland Point.

This flat expanse is what geologists call a raised beach. The original coastline ran at the foot of the cliffs, seen rising over 200 feet (60m) some distance inland. The theory is that the beach assumed its present level when relieved of the pressure of the ice that retreated at the end of the Ice Age.

If planning to cross the Helford River by ferry during Oct.–Mar. (See Section 45), check now by phone that the ferry service is available. Contact Cove Boats tel: (01326) 250116, or the Ferry Boat Inn, Helford Passage tel: (01326) 250116. Alternative: local weekday bus Coverack–Helston: connections to Falmouth.

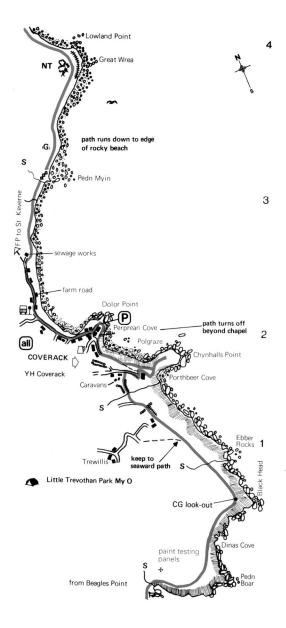

61

Section 44
LOWLAND POINT–
NARE POINT
4¼ miles (6¾km); easy
Cum. 179 miles (288km)

From Lowland Point the Path follows the coastline to Dean Quarry. Follow carefully the sign-posted route through the busy quarry workings, down to the beach at Godrevy Cove. Immediately look for the stream at the exit from the beach. In the field, walk with the hedge on the right up to Rosenithon Farm and then to Porthoustock and Porthallow.

A mile (1½km) out to sea from Dean Quarry are the Manacles, the most dangerous reefs on the south Cornish coast. Lying not far from the shipping lanes in and out of Falmouth, they have claimed thousands of victims. Among the most tragic losses was that of *HMS Dispatch* bringing back troops from Corunna in 1809 — wrecked here on the same night as *HMS Primrose*. Only eight survived. The emigrant ship, *John*, in May 1855 and the *Mohegan* in October 1898, both bound for the USA, also suffered appalling losses.

An alternative route takes you from Rosenithon inland to St Keverne, ¾ mile (1km) away. It has shops and two pubs. A good footpath leads from there down to Porthallow.

Many shipwreck victims are buried in the churchyard of St Keverne. The Three Tuns Inn probably got its name from the three tuns of smuggled French wine that a 15th-century vicar is said to have concealed.

Porthallow is a pleasing village. The Five Pilchards pub displays interesting pictures of the Manacles wrecks. From Porthallow, the Coast Path is once again a clear track following the cliff closely past the large mass of Nare Head and beyond Nare Point. There is an enjoyable view from Nare Point over the wooded Helford River estuary and Falmouth Bay.

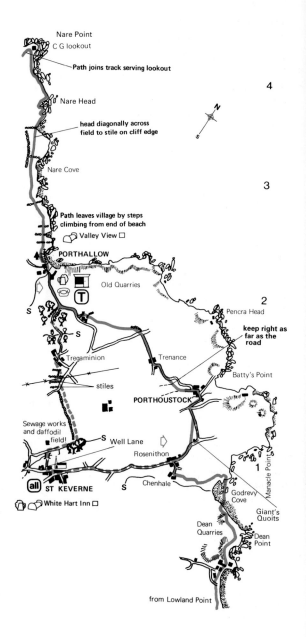

Section 45

NARE POINT-
HELFORD PASSAGE

5 miles (8km); easy

Cum. 184 miles (296km)

The Path drops down to the south bank of the small inlet, Gillan Creek. In Gillan a sign directs you along a private road parallel to and finishing on the shore of the creek. There is no ferry but the creek can be waded within one hour each side of low tide (see map). If you miss low tide, take the road turning inland by Gillan Cove House. On reaching the public road, turn left then turn right at the T-junction with phone box. Continue past the large house (Carne) and round the head of the creek down the north shore to the delightful hamlet of St Anthony. No shops or refreshment at Gillan, Flushing or St Anthony but there are at Manaccan — see below.

St Anthony's church has a Norman nave and chancel but the oak roof is 15th-century.

The Path continues behind the church, through the private Bosahan estate (dogs prohibited), right round to Helford via Dennis Head (Dinas meaning 'fort'), the site of an Iron Age cliff castle. The Path is a clear track through thick woods along the south bank of the Helford Inlet to Helford, a most attractive former smugglers' haunt. Refreshments available at either The Shipwright's Arms or Rose Cottage. The ferry across Helford river runs on request, tide and weather permitting (Easter-Oct. 9.30am-5.30pm). See Section 43 for an alternative when the ferry is not operating.

For a pleasing short-cut from Gillan Creek to Helford, continue straight on after Carne (not round the creek). After a short distance, take the footpath on the right through a wood to Manaccan. The Norman church, which was restored last century has a 14th-century tower. A footpath on the left of the village street takes you down to Helford.

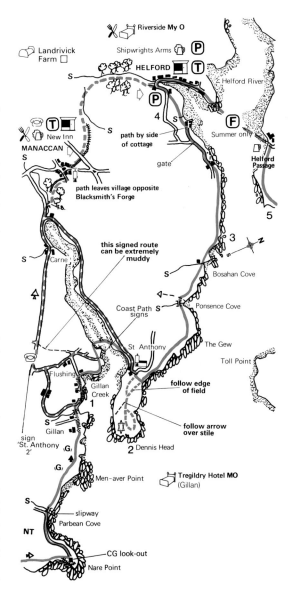

Section 46
HELFORD PASSAGE-FALMOUTH

6½ miles (10½km); moderate
Cum. 190½ miles (306½km)

The Path runs clearly along the north shore of the Helford River estuary. After a few minutes you arrive at the little hamlet of Durgan.

Durgan, with its few cottages, looks idyllic in its setting of trees and water. A favourite anchorage for small boats, it was traditionally, as far back as Roman times, a busy deep-water haven for trading vessels from as far away as the Mediterranean. An old pack-horse track running north-west from Durgan provides a right of way to the Mawnan-Helford Passage road and to Glendurgan, ½ mile (¾km) inland from Durgan, a garden property of the National Trust, with fine trees and shrubs, such as rhododendrons and azaleas and a laurel maze. Open Mar.-Oct., Mon., Wed. and Fri. (except Good Friday) 10.30am-5.30pm. Parking nearby.

Next on the Path is the Mawnan Shear headland and Parson's Beach (National Trust).

In the hamlet of Mawnan, the church of St Mawnan-in-Meneage (Meneage rhymes with vague and in Cornish means 'land of monks') stands in an oval Celtic entrenchment. Mainly 15th-century, it is dedicated to St Maunanus, a 6th-century Welsh missionary monk. The village of Mawnan Smith, 1¼ miles (2km) inland, has an old thatched pub, The Red Lion. Bus service weekdays to Falmouth.

The Path rounds Rosemullion Head and continues near the cliff edge, past inviting coves, down towards Falmouth, via Maen Porth and on to Pennance Point. From here it is 1½ miles (2½km) by the Path to Swanpool Beach and Point, the outskirts of Falmouth, dealt with separately on p.13.

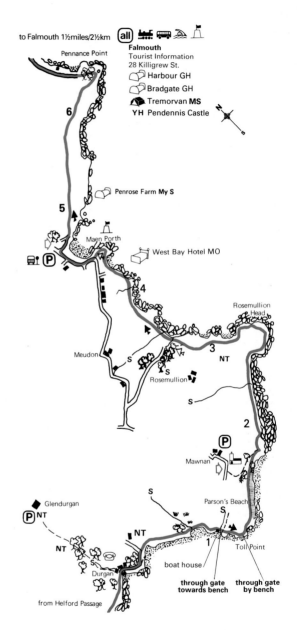

to Falmouth 1½miles/2½km

Falmouth
Tourist Information
28 Killigrew St.
Harbour GH
Bradgate GH
Tremorvan **MS**
YH Pendennis Castle

Pennance Point

6

Penrose Farm **My S**

5

Maen Porth

West Bay Hotel MO

4

Rosemullion Head

Meudon

3 **NT**

S

Rosemullion

S

2

Mawnan

S

Parson's Beach

Glendurgan

NT

NT

NT

boat house

1

Toll Point

Durgan

from Helford Passage

through gate towards bench **through gate by bench**

Section 47
PLACE–PORTSCATHO
5½ miles (8¾km); easy
Cum. 196 miles (315½km)

From Falmouth, there is a regular ferry to St Mawes, daily May-mid Oct. Last departure about 5pm. Service less frequent mid Oct.-Apr., weekdays only. Last departure about 4pm.

At the time of writing, there is a ferry (May-Sept) between St. Mawes and Place. Otherwise, the F&B Boat Co. (tel: 01209-214901) will take passengers by prior arrangement. There is a local bus service (weekdays) from St. Mawes to Portscatho (p. 66). To walk from St. Mawes via the A3078, it is 8 miles (13km) to Place or, alternatively, 4½ miles (7¼km) direct to Portscatho.

St Mawes (from the Irish saint, Machatus) is well-known as a yachting centre. All facilities for food and accommodation. The castle is a 16th-century fort and can be visited daily.

The Manor House in Place stands on the site of a 13th-century monastery. The adjoining church of St Anthony in Roseland has some 13th-century features.

The Path from Place is signposted behind the church and climbs along a field, drops to the shore and turns west before rounding St Anthony's Head with fine views. There is a lighthouse on the Head. The Path drops gradually through fields almost to the water's edge, past Porthbeor Beach (no swimming) to Towan Beach — a quiet, sandy bathing beach owned by the National Trust. There is a car park at Porth Farm from where a short path leads to the beach.

The Path continues along the low cliff with views over Portscatho, another attractive fishing village.

The Plume of Feathers is a good pub. There are facilities for food and accommodation (see p.66) and a local bus service to Truro on certain days.

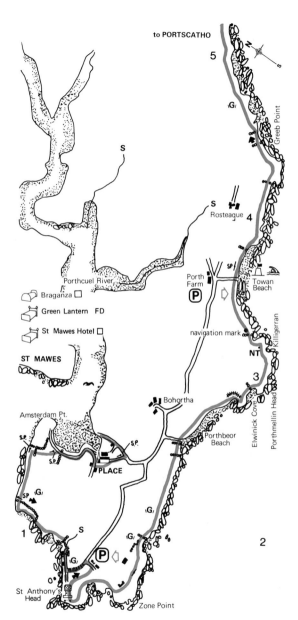

Section 48

PORTSCATHO–NARE HEAD

4¼ miles (6¾km); strenuous

Cum. 200¼ miles (322¼km)

The Path leads northwards along North Parade, down to the small Porthcurnick Beach and then continues past the Coast Guard look-out.

When the Path reaches Creek Stephen Point there is a footpath inland to Curgurrel and the main A3078 road. Near the junction is a large earthwork called Dingerein Castle (Dinas Gerein meaning 'Geraint's Castle'). Geraint is mentioned in the Anglo-Saxon Chronicle as a King of the Britons in the 8th century.

On from Creek Stephen Point, the Path hugs the coast until, after a diversion inland at an hotel, it leads to Pendower Beach, popular in summer. Refreshments are available in season. Another diversion inland by road, to avoid landslides, leads down to the Path. Alternatively you can cross the beach when tide allows.

The stretch from Pendower Beach to Nare Head is exacting. Rough in parts, there are some steep climbs as the 330-foot (101m) Nare Head is approached. The extensive views in all directions are worth the effort. The landscape inland is a pleasant one of pasture and growing crops with patches of woodland.

Inland from Nare Head rises the tumulus-crowned Carne Beacon which is 340 feet (104m) high. The walk from the Beacon to Nare Head is on National Trust land. There is a small car park with access to the Coast Path at the hamlet of Carne.

For those walking east-west and planning to cross to St Mawes and Falmouth, there may be a ferry May-Sept; otherwise the F&B Boat Co. (tel: 01209 214901) will take passengers across by prior arrangement. Alternatively there is a weekday bus service Portscatho to St. Mawes. To walk Portscatho to St. Mawes is 4½ miles (7¼km) or to St. Mawes from Place is 8 miles (13km).

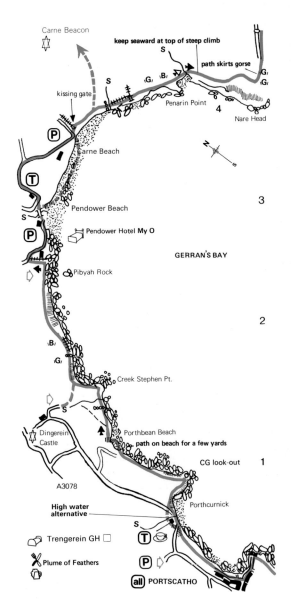

Section 49

NARE HEAD-PORTLOE-
PORTHOLLAND

3¼ miles (5¼km); strenuous

Cum. 203½ miles (327½km)

From Nare Head to Portloe you are on National Trust territory for almost all of the way. Following its usual practice, the Trust has ensured that the Path is clear to follow. There are one or two stiff climbs as you pass Kiberick Cove and Manare Point.

Portloe is a delightful small fishing cove which looks very much the same as it would have 50 or more years ago. There is only very limited public parking space and this keeps it relatively quiet and unspoiled. The 17th-century Lugger Hotel, right on the diminutive slip-way, must have originally been a pub. There is also The Ship Inn which offers accommodation. The hotel, the inn, a post office stores and a few cottages comprise Portloe.

Gull Rock ½ mile (¾km) off Nare Head is a favourite nesting-place for sea-birds: herring gulls, cormorants, shags, kittiwakes, guillemots and razorbills. It has also taken its toll of shipping — the last sailing ship to be wrecked there was the 2,000-ton *Hera* in February 1914 with the loss of 19, including the captain.

The Path climbs out of the village street of Portloe up some steep steps leading to the Coast Guard look-out on the cliff. It then keeps very close to the edge of the cliffs that drop sheer to the sea. The effect is magnificent. Portholland (West and East) has two small sandy beaches. There is a post-office stores which supplies snack food in the summer.

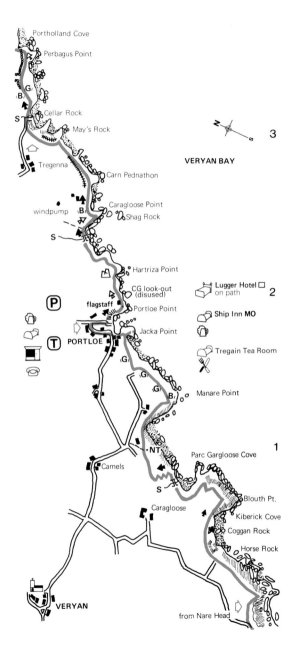

Section 50

PORTHOLLAND COVE–
DODMAN POINT

4¾ miles (7¾km); moderate

Cum. 208¼ miles (335km)

From Portholland Cove the Path is easy to follow leading on to a metalled track. On reaching the edge of the cliff above Porthluney Cove, you turn inland and follow the road for about 300 yards (275m) down to the beach.

Porthluney Cove is a popular wide sandy beach. The refreshment booth is open in summer. The beach, which provides good safe swimming, is in a beautiful setting of wood, stream and pasture with Caerhays Castle as a centrepiece. The Castle was built in 1808 by John Nash on the site of a much older manor house. The film *Rebecca* was shot here. The Castle can be visited on certain days of the year.

You will need to keep on the road for a short way to regain the Path. You will see the kissing-gate on the roadside; take the track running up across a field, then over the stile and keep to the seaward boundary of the next field. You climb up steadily, through a copse and emerge above the bay bounded on the east by Greeb Point, with fine views ahead of you. Eventually you will reach the quiet, sandy Hemmick Beach. There are no refreshment facilities, except, perhaps, for an occasional ice-cream van.

There is parking at Penare ½ mile (¾km) up the road running east from the beach. The Boswinger Youth Hostel is ½ mile (¾km) up the road running west from the beach.

From Hemmick Beach the Path rises steadily to the 370-foot (112m) summit of Dodman Point, with its cross, erected in 1896 by the Rector of St Michael Caerhays as a guide to seafarers. There is also a small disused Coast Guard refuge. Dropping down from the Point, care is needed.

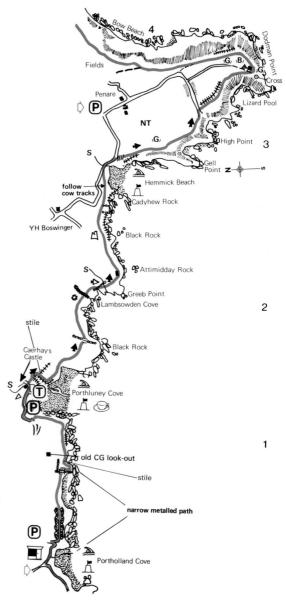

68

Section 51
DODMAN POINT-
MEVAGISSEY

4¾ miles (7¾km); moderate
Cum. 213 miles (342¾km)

The Path down from Dodman Point eventually follows a clearly defined track round the fine shingle Bow or Vault Beach, which can be reached by footpath. The route continues down to Gorran Haven passing a Coast Guard look-out. Gorran Haven has a small harbour. There is an inn situated in the more modern part of the town. The bus service to Mevagissey runs Mon.-Fri.

The Gwineas Rocks, 1 mile (1½km) off Gorran Haven have caused many shipwrecks, one large vessel as recently as 1940.

The long Great Perhaven Beach of sand and rocks lies north-east of Gorran Haven and the Path provides access to it. You can bathe in selected spots.

Above Turbot Beach, there is a field known as Bodrugan's Leap. Sir Henry Treworth, from nearby Bodrugan, when fleeing from Bosworth in 1485, took refuge in his home. He was pursued and had to make a spectacular leap on his horse to the beach, where a boat was waiting to take him to France.

Portmellon has a small bathing beach. The route to Mevagissey is by road, a rather uncomfortable walk in summer traffic.

Mevagissey: the name probably derived from the names of two early saints: St Mewan or Meva or St Ida or Issey. Formerly one of Cornwall's busiest fishing ports, it is now dependent on the holiday trade. The church is 15th-century with Norman parts. Mevagissey offers good fishing, including shark-fishing. Food, accommodation and parking facilities are available and there is a weekday bus service to Gorran Haven and St Austell. The two pubs are The Fountain and The Ship. The town is very crowded in summer.

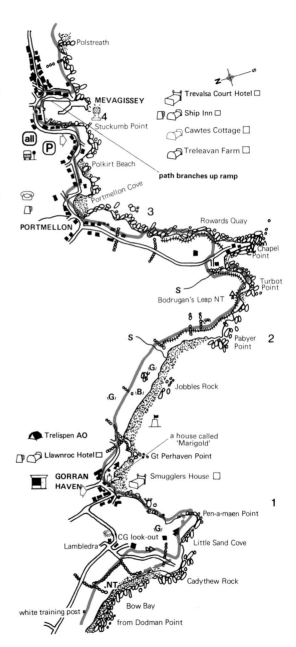

69

Section 52

MEVAGISSEY–PENTEWAN–PORTHPEAN

4 miles (6½km); strenuous
Cum. 217 miles (349¼km)

The Path climbs above the harbour of Mevagissey, passes Polstreath, rounds Penare Point and then drops down alongside the busy main road and the caravans of Pentewan Sands. At the bottom of the slope, turn right off the main road, cross the stream and you are in Pentewan with pub, shops and parking.

For the official route of the Coast Path, go through the village and take Pentewan Hill that rises steeply to the left. Continue for 100 yds up the hill and turn right along the Terrace. At the end of the Terrace, the Coast Path starts between barbed-wire fences but soon widens, proceeding along the crest of the cliffs. The Path continues, involving two steep combes before dropping down to Hallane and the cottage below. A convenient stop for a rest but no facilities available.

Turn up the cart track from the beach for a short way. The Path continues through a gate on the right, rising until it crosses the neck of Black Head, an impressive promontory. You can divert to enjoy fine views of the coast.

Where the Path emerges on to a minor road, turn right and in a few steps, after a fork, there is a small parking place on the right. Leading out of the far end of this space, up some steps, the Path continues through a field. There are two steep combes to negotiate on the stretch to Porthpean. At Porthpean, there is a restaurant and refreshments are available in the summer. No facilities, including car park, out of season.

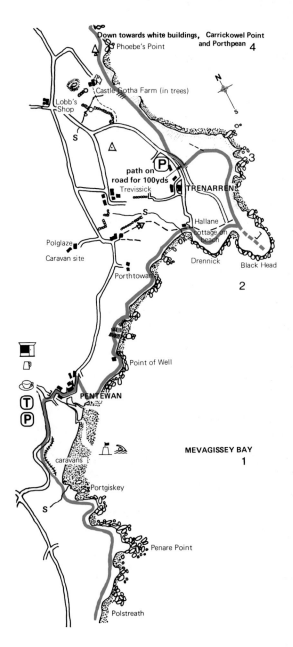

Section 53

PORTHPEAN-CHARLESTOWN-
SPIT POINT

3½ miles (5½km); easy

Cum. 220½ miles (354¾km)

*From Porthpean, the Path climbs up from
the beach through pine woods and continues
along the cliff. You emerge eventually above
a beach, which is reserved for the nearby
holiday camp, and drop down to Charlestown,
an attractive little port.*

Charlestown is named after Charles
Rashleigh, one of the influential
Rashleigh family from Menabilly near
Fowey. He built the port in 1791 to handle
ore from the mines but soon the working
of china-clay replaced the mining of ore.
Fowey and Par became more important
as shippers of china-clay and
Charlestown declined. There is a
weekday bus service to St Austell, Par
and Fowey. You can cross the harbour
entrance over the lock gate.

*From Charlestown, the Path continues
over springy turf along the cliff-top, behind
gardens of houses, passing in front of the
imposing Carlyon Hotel and, from there,
follows the seaward boundary of the golf
course. Below is the long, sandy Crinnis
Beach with the large Cornwall Coliseum
complex.*

There are weekday bus services to St
Austell and Par.

*Beyond Crinnis Beach, the Path descends
to just above the foreshore, leading to Spit
Point and the unattractive china-clay
installations which have dominated the scene
for most of this stretch. Traversing this area
can hardly be called pleasant but can, perhaps,
be regarded as a necessary link with more
attractive country further on.*

*Those walking east-west will find the exit
from Porthpean at the end of the promenade,
signposted on the seaward side of the green
shelter.*

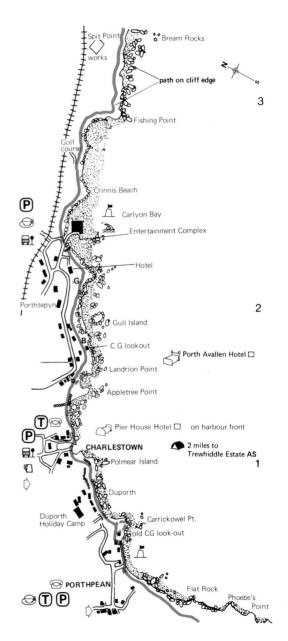

Section 54
SPIT POINT–PAR–FOWEY
6 miles (9¾km); moderate
Cum. 226½ miles (364½km)

At Spit Point, you come to the boundary of the English China Clays Ltd. works. The Path turns inland along the fence, through part of the works, to the main road (A3082). Turn right (east) along the road. You now have a walk of 1¼ miles (2km) through built-up areas, to the entrance of the huge Par Sands Caravan site. Just beyond, where the road turns inland, is the continuation of the Coastal Path. Alternatively, there is a weekday bus service along this road. Ask to be dropped at the Par Sands entrance of the caravan site.

The Path runs along the low cliff fringing Par Sands. Narrow in places, it continues between the cliff-edge and pasture land down to Polkerris, an unspoiled fishing cove with a little harbour and small sandy beach.

Facilities include stores and restored pub, The Rashleigh Arms. Above the harbour are the ruins of a 300-year-old fish cellar where pilchards were salted and stored.

From the road, near the harbour, the Path climbs steeply through a wood before emerging on to fields along the cliff-top. A pleasant 2-mile (3¼km) walk brings you to the 250-foot (75m) Gribbin Head (National Trust) with its 80-foot (25m) day-mark. The descent, providing charming views of cliff, wood and pasture, brings you to the sandy beach of Polridmouth (known as 'Pridmouth') with safe bathing but there are no refreshment or other facilities.

Menabilly House, ½ mile (¾km) inland, was the seat of the Rashleigh family for 400 years. Daphne du Maurier lived here and this was the setting of her novel *Rebecca*. The house is not visible through the trees and cannot be visited.

The Path leads up from Polridmouth through a little wood above the beach. Keep to the cliff edge and you emerge above Coombe Hawne, very near Fowey.

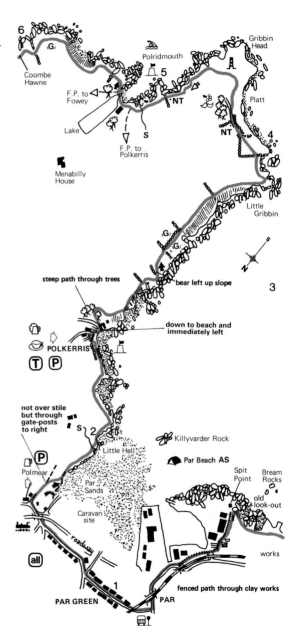

Section 55

FOWEY–LANTIVET BAY

3¾ miles (6km); strenuous

Cum. 230¼ miles (370½km)

Coming round the headland into the fields above the Fowey estuary, the Path descends through the wood to Readymoney Cove on the outskirts of Fowey.

Just off the Path to the right are the remains of St Catherine's Castle built by Henry VIII as a fort to defend the harbour.

If walking east-west from Polruan, turn left (south-west) from the ferry, along the Esplanade leading to Readymoney Cove. The Path goes up into the woods between two cottages on the far side of the beach.

Fowey (pronounced 'Foy'), a most attractive town, was granted its charter in 1245, supplying ships for many mediaeval campaigns as well as privateering on the side. John Rashleigh's ship *Francis of Foye* accompanied Drake and Raleigh on their voyages and fought against the Armada. The Ship Inn, formerly the 16th-century town house of the Rashleigh's was the Roundhead headquarters during the Civil War. The town has a bus service to Par and St Austell. There is a regular daily ferry service to Polruan on the opposite bank of the estuary. The car ferry to Bodinnick which is ½ mile (¾km) up-river, runs daily from 8am to 9pm or dusk. The museum and the 15th-century church of St Finbarrus may be of interest.

For the Coast Path, cross to Polruan. Turn right on leaving the quay and follow the street along the waterfront. Turn sharp left up the last street on your left (Battery Lane). The route continues in the same direction, skirting the town, joining the Coast Path near a car park. Alternatively, you can follow the main road up through the town from the quay, joining the Path by the car park. There are some steep climbs but the next 7 miles (11¼km) is judged one of the best walks on the coast.

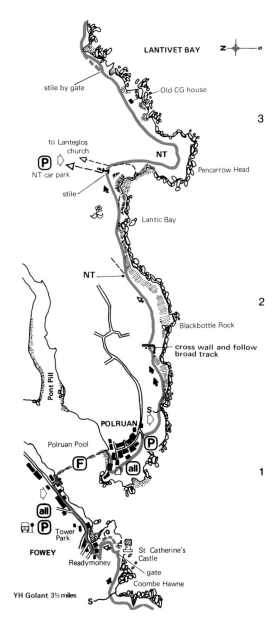

73

Section 56

LANTIVET BAY–POLPERRO

3½ miles (5½km); strenuous

Cum. 233¾ miles (376¼km)

From Lantivet Bay, the bracken-covered slopes reach down nearly to the water's edge as does the Path. Wild flowers flourish here, including some rarities. The Path continues steeply down to West Coombe, where there is another beach with patches of sand among the rocks, a real smuggler's cove.

A track leads inland from West Coombe to the hamlet of Lansallos which has a farm, a few houses and the 15th-century church of St Ildierna. There is a National Trust car park where refreshment can be obtained.

The Path continues through National Trust land, the boundary being the next stream. From the stream, the Path climbs the slope ahead, passing a white-painted navigation aid marking the Udder Rock, 1 mile (1½km) off-shore where you can also make out a buoy. There are fine views from this part of the Path. Shortly after, the Path descends sharply through the bracken to a small stream, with a hard climb the other side. You come to the summit of a small headland above the off-shore rock, The Larrick, which is almost covered at high tide. Here, you drop sharply down. After another climb and descent you again enter National Trust land by taking 150 steps up to a wide cliff path, with fine views, for 1 mile (1½km) into Polperro.

Polperro is the picture-book old Cornish village — white-washed cottages and narrow streets, all rather spoiled by summer crowds. Best seen in the off-season or after 6pm when the parties have left for home. Cars are prohibited in the village in the summer; parking is available ¾ mile (1km) inland. There are facilities for food and accommodation as well as many shops and a local daily bus service to Looe but no Sunday service out of season.

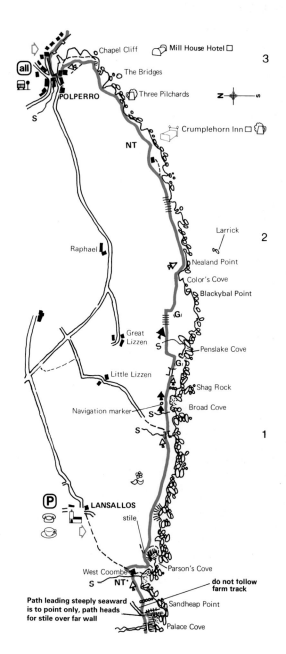

74

Section 57

POLPERRO-LOOE

4½ miles (7¼km); moderate

Cum. 238¼ miles (383½km)

For Looe, follow the narrow street up from the east end of Polperro harbour which brings you out on to the Coast Path. The walk follows a well marked cliff-path through The Warren and on to Talland Bay and its small sandy beach. Refreshments are available but parking space is limited.

Just inland is the hamlet of Porthallow and on the hill ½ mile (¾km) to the east is the 13th-century church of Talland Barton.

From Talland the Path follows the coastline on the fringe of the West Looe Down, which is pleasant open pastureland sloping from 300 feet (90m) down to the sea. Shortly after leaving Talland, you will see two high landmarks which denote one end of a nautical mile for naval speed trials.

After rounding Portnadler Bay and, about 2 miles (3¼km) from Talland, the Path enters Looe at Marine Drive, a promenade with large houses on the landward side, which leads to West Looe and the bridge across the Looe River.

On the Downs just before you get to Marine Drive, you can see the foundations of the ancient Celtic Chapel of Lammanna. The caves of Looe Island or St Georges, ½ mile (¾km) off Hannafore Point, were put to good use by smugglers. The island is now a bird reserve and boat trips leave for the island from Looe.

Looe (pop. 5,000) is a popular resort. Until 1832, West and East Looe were two separate communities and each sent two members to Parliament. Both communities were granted charters in the 13th century and were important fishing ports with smuggling as a sideline. Looe has two beaches, a museum, two mediaeval churches and a railway station. Two old pubs: The Jolly Sailors (W. Looe) and The Fisherman's Arms (E. Looe).

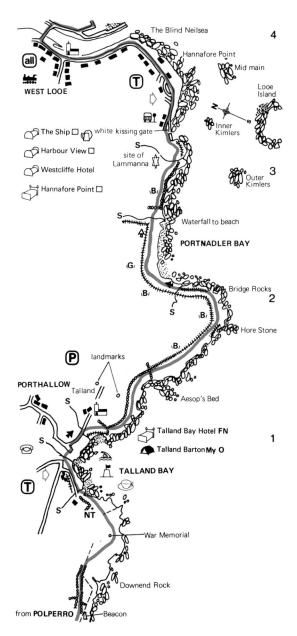

75

Section 58

LOOE–SEATON

3½ miles (5½km); easy

Cum. 241¾ miles (389km)

After you have crossed the bridge connecting East Looe to West Looe, turn south toward the harbour mouth. There is also a local ferry nearer the harbour mouth which avoids the trudge inland to the bridge. You will find the post office and the 16th-century Guildhall with information office in Fore Street, Looe's main street. A few steps further, on the opposite side to the Guildhall, is Castle Street, rising steeply. You turn up here — there is a sign to Plaidy and Millendreath — and the street brings you to the East Cliff footpath from where there is a good view of the beach, harbour and Hannafore on the other side.

This is now the Coast Path, which continues partly on footpath and road through the villas of Plaidy to Millendreath.

Millendreath Beach is a colony of chalets which, for once, do not offend the eye. There is a sandy beach, refreshments and a shop.

From the beach you take the steep lane on the right (can be muddy), following the line of the cliffs. After about ½mile (¾km) there is Bodigga Farm on the left. The Coast Path turns off on the right from the lane after a short distance. The Path eventually joins the main road above Seaton.

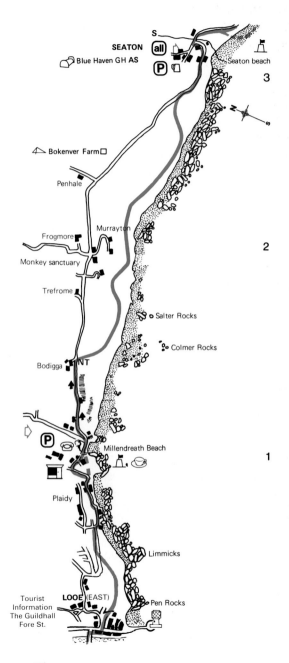

76

Section 59

SEATON-DOWNDERRY-
PORTWRINKLE

3½ miles (5½km); easy

Cum. 245¼ miles (394¾km)

Seaton has a beach of grey sand and pebbles and a large caravan site. There are facilities for food and accommodation, an inn and a weekday bus service to Looe and Plymouth.

From Seaton for the next 10 miles (16km) the route of the Coast Path can hardly be called enjoyable, much of it being on the road. There is, in parts, an alternative route along the beach but, even here, activity on the army firing range can put you back on the road. You would be excused if you chose the bus all the way to Plymouth but then you would miss Rame Head and Cawsand, both attractive spots.

From Seaton to Downderry you can choose between the beach above the high tide mark or the road.

Downderry, perched on the cliff with houses lining the road, has all facilities for refreshment and accommodation, with shops, parking and The Ship Inn, with a cliff-top garden. The beach below is sand and shingle. There is a weekday bus service to Looe and Plymouth.

From Downderry, keep on the road for a short way until, at a hairpin bend, the Path follows a field boundary over the Battern Cliffs for ¾ mile (1¼km) before joining the road again.

At the time of writing there is no defined footpath to Portwrinkle and you should, therefore, keep to the road. An official path may be sign-posted as such by the time this guide is printed.

Portwrinkle is a little former fishing port with a small sandy beach. There is a licensed hotel on the hill behind the port.

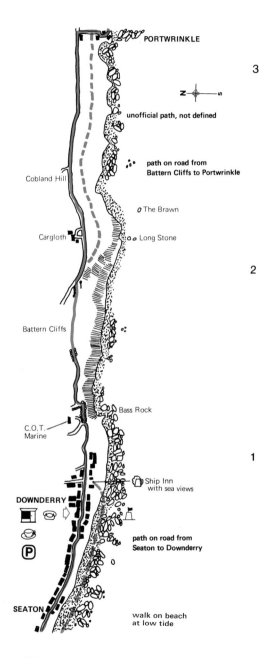

PORTWRINKLE

3

unofficial path, not defined

path on road from
Battern Cliffs to Portwrinkle

Cobland Hill

o The Brawn

2

Cargloth

o o Long Stone

Battern Cliffs

Bass Rock

C.O.T.
Marine

1

Ship Inn
with sea views

DOWNDERRY

path on road from
Seaton to Downderry

SEATON

walk on beach
at low tide

Section 60
PORTWRINKLE-FREATHY
3¾ miles (6km); moderate
Cum. 249 miles(400¾km)

Take the road running along the low cliff at Portwrinkle and, where it turns inland, starting the ascent towards Crafthole, the drive to the hotel and golf club house will be seen on the left (north). Opposite this drive entrance is the Coast Path once again, taking you to the cliff top. The Path follows the seaward boundary of the golf course for nearly 1 mile (1½km) and then turns inland to the road.

Where the Path leaves the cliff to turn inland, another path (not clearly marked) turns off seaward, descending steeply to the beach of Whitsand Bay below Trethill Cliffs (National Trust).

Whitsand Bay, a fine stretch of sand almost 3 miles (5km) long is deceptive. Firstly, because of strong currents, bathing is dangerous and, secondly, there is an army range on Tregantle Cliff, 1 mile (1½km) along the beach. Red flags are hoisted when firing is in progress and access to the sands is forbidden at such times. There are no facilities for refreshment anywhere along here.

If the tide allows — and it comes in swiftly — and there is no firing, you can walk along the sands, even as far as Polhawn Cove (see Section 61). Otherwise take the road, as mentioned above, to Freathy. There is a bus service to Plymouth on weekdays. If you walk on the beach, the cliffs will hide from you an unattractive view of the village of Freathy.

Whitsand Bay was the scene of many shipwrecks in the days of sail when gales drove vessels off course when trying to make Plymouth Sound. 'Reception committees' of local residents often took everything of value from both vessels and victims — but there are also tales of heroic rescues.

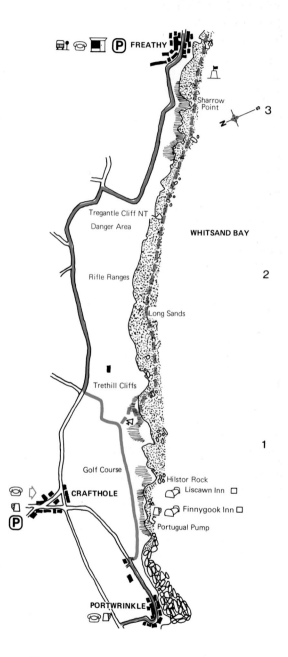

78

Section 61

FREATHY-RAME HEAD-
PENLEE POINT

4¾ miles (7¾km); easy

Cum. 253¾ miles (408¼km)

Walk along the cliff road or along the sands of Whitsand Bay until you reach the junction with the road inland to Wiggle, where the Coast Path resumes on the right (south). A steep path leads down to the Cove itself. To avoid the walk along the road or the sands there is a weekday bus service along the cliff road between Freathy and Cawsand. If you wish to walk round Rame Head, ask for Polhawn.

On the cliff as you leave Freathy by road, there is a memorial to a drowned son from his family, a reminder of the danger of bathing in the bay.

The Path continues from the old fort on a well-defined track over the turf towards Rame Head, with fine views over the Bay. The Head is 300 feet (90m) high and guards the western entrance to Plymouth Sound. The ruined chapel on the summit was dedicated to St Michael in 1397. Turning easterly, the Path passes seaward of the Coast Guard station to Penlee Point and its Grotto, a former look-out.

For an alternative route to Cawsand on foot if you do not have time to walk round Rame Head, you can take the footpath on the left (north-east) of the cliff road about ½ mile (¾km) beyond the memorial. This brings you to Treninnow Farm from where a quiet road runs to Cawsand.

The church tower, seen inland as you walk, is that of the hamlet of Rame. The church was dedicated to St Germanus. Mainly 15th-century, it was first mentioned 1,000 years ago.

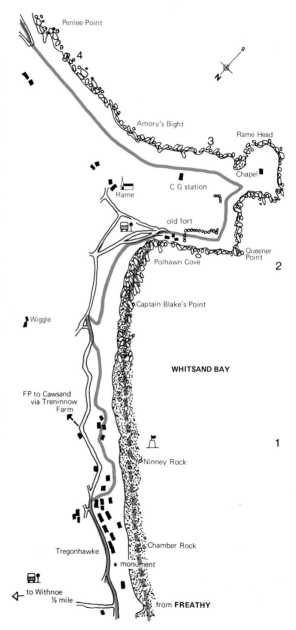

Penlee Point

Amory's Bight

Rame Head

Chapel

C G station

Rame

old fort

Queener Point

Polhawn Cove

2

Captain Blake's Point

Wiggle

WHITSAND BAY

FP to Cawsand
via Treninnow
Farm

1

Ninney Rock

Tregonhawke

Chamber Rock

monument

to Withnoe
½ mile

from FREATHY

Section 62

PENLEE POINT-
CAWSAND-CREMYLL

4½ miles (7¼km); easy

Cum. 258¼ miles (415½km)

From Penlee Point the Coast Path continues for 1¼ miles (2km) along a metalled track through woods to Cawsand.

The twin fishing villages of Cawsand and Kingsand date back to the Middle Ages. Life here, for the busiest smugglers in the west, was a continual battle with Customs. Local girls took brandy into Plymouth under their petticoats and Harry Carter (see p.54) was nearly captured off Cawsand. There is a weekday bus service to Cremyll (for Plymouth) and a launch service in summer to Plymouth (Mayflower Steps). There are beaches in both Kingsand and Cawsand.

For the Path to Cremyll, go up Cawsand's main street and through Kingsand. Pass the rising Sun Inn, go through the field gate on the right of the Mount Edgcumbe Country Park. Having passed the house, Hooe Pool, cross the stile and keep on until you enter the woods by an iron gate.

The path inland up the slope leads to the ancient Maker church, the tower of which was used for years as a naval signal station. This more level path is a shorter alternative to Cremyll.

The Path descends, passing Lady Emma's Cottage — Nelson's lady stayed there — emerging below the impressive Mount Edgcumbe mansion.

The original Tudor mansion, seat of a famous Cornish family, was destroyed in the Plymouth blitz of 1941 but has been completely restored. The park and gardens are open all the year round; the house is open in summer. For times, ring (01752) 26489.

Cremyll is the terminal of the ferry, running regularly since the 1200s to and from Plymouth. For first and last ferry times, ring (01752) 822105

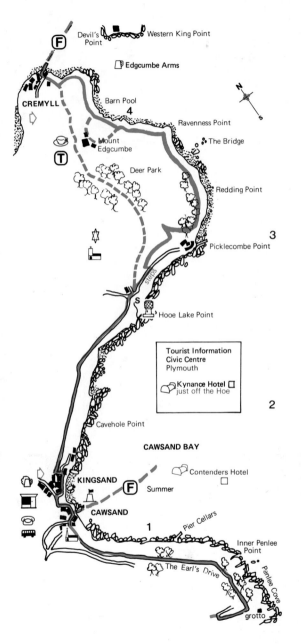

80